TOP TITLES and TIPS TOO!

FOR ALL OF LIFE'S COMMON AND NOT-SO-COMMON SCRAPBOOK TOPICS
BY CRYSTAL DAWN PERRY

For all of life's common and not-so-common scrapbook topics
By Crystal Dawn Perry

Top Titles and Tips Too!
ClearSky Publishing
P.O. Box 606-B Hixson, TN. 37343

www.clearskyday.com

Copyright c2007 ClearSky Publishing
All Rights Reserved. No part of this product may be reproduced or distributed in any form including commercial purposes or by electronic means. Law strictly forbids distribution without prior written permission of the publisher. With purchase, permission is granted to reproduce verses from this book, on a limited basis, for personal use only.
Printed in the United States of America.

Top Titles & Tips Too!
978-0-9706381-6-8

I dedicate this book to my incredibly incredible family.

Table of Contents

a

Adoption	1
Airplane	1
Amusement Park	2
Angel	3
Animal	4
Anniversary	4
Ant	5
Apple	5
Archery	6
Armed Forces	6
Art	6
Attitude	7
Aunt	8
Autumn	8

B

Baby	9
Baking	10
Ball	11
Baptism/Christening/Church	11
Baseball	12
Basketball	13
Bathtime	14
Beach	15
Beauty	17
Bee	17
Bicycle	18
Birds	19
Birthday	20
Blocks	21

Boat/Cruise 22
Book 23
Bowling 24
Boxing 24
Boy/Boys 24
Boyfriend 25
Boy Scouts 26
Break-Up 26
Brother 27
Bubble Bath/Bubbles 28
Bug 29
Bus 30
Butterfly 30

C

Cake 31
Camping 31
Candy/Chocolate 32
Car 33
Carousel 33
Cat 34
Chalk 35
Cheerleader 35
Cherry 36
Chicken 36
Child/Children 37
Christmas 38
Circle 40
Circus 40
Clothing 40
Clouds 41
Clown 41
College 41
Color/Coloring 42

Computer 42
Construction 43
Cooking 44
Cookout 45
Country 45
Cousin 46
Cow 46
Cowboy 47
Crafts 48
Crawling 48
Crocodile 49
Crying 49
Cut 50
Cute 50

D

Daddy 51
Dance 52
Date 52
Daughter 53
Death 53
Diet 54
Dinosaur 55
Dirty/Messy 55
Divorce 56
Doctor 56
Dog 57
Do-it-Yourself/Remodeling 58
Doll 59
Dreams 59
Dress-up/Style 60
Driving 61
Drums 63

e

Ears 63
Earth 63
Easter 64
Eating 65
Engagement 67
Exercise 68
Everyday Life 68
Eyes 69

F

Fairytale 70
Fall 71
Family 73
Family Tree 74
Farm 74
Father 75
Father-in-Law 76
Feet 76
Fight/Fighting 77
Fire 78
Firsts 79
Fish/Fishing 79
Flower 80
Football 82
Friend 82
Frog 84
Four-Wheeling 84

g

Gambling 85
Games 86
Gardening 86
Gifts 87

Girl/Girls	88
Girlfriend	89
Girl Scouts	90
Glasses	90
Golf	91
Graduation	91
Grandchildren	92
Grandfather	93
Grandmother	93
Grandparents	95
Grow/Growing	95
Gymnastics	97

H

Habit	97
Hair	98
Halloween	99
Hand	100
Handmade	101
Hanukkah	101
Happiness	102
Harvest	103
Hat	103
Heart	103
Heaven	104
Heritage	105
Hiking	106
Hockey	107
Home/House	107
Home School	109
Horse	109
Hug	110
Hunting	111

i

Ice Cream 112
Illness 112
Independence Day/Patriotism 113
Injury 114
Inspirational 116

j

Job 116
Jumping 116

k

Kindergarten 117
Kiss 118
Kite 119
Knot 119

l

Laugh/Laughing/Laughter 120
Love 120

m

Magic 122
Make-believe 123
Martial Arts 123
Memories 124
Men 125
Military 125
Milk 127
Money 127
Monkey 128
Moon 129
Mother 129
Mother-in-Law 130

Motorcycle 130
Movies/Television 131
Multiples 132
Music 134

n

Name 135
Nature 136
Neighbor 136
Newspaper 137
New Year 137
Noah's Ark 138
Nude 138

o

Odor 139

p

Park 139
Party 140
Passover 141
Peach 141
Pet 141
Photographs/Photography 144
Piano 144
Picnic 145
Pie 145
Pig 145
Pirate 146
Play/Program 146
Pool 146
Pregnancy 147
Prom 147
Pumpkin 148

r

Rabbit 149
Race/Racing 149
Puzzle 149
Rafting 150
Rain 151
Rainbow 152
Retirement 152
Reunion 153
Rock/Rocking Chair 154
Rolling Over 154
Run/Running 155

s

Sad 156
Santa Claus 156
Scare 157
School 158
Scrapbooking 160
Sewing 161
Shine 161
Shoe 162
Shopping 162
Shower 162
Sibling 164
Sick 165
Silly 165
Sister 165
Skate 166
Skateboard 166
Skiing 167
Sleep 168
Slide 170
Smile 170

Snake	171
Snow/Winter	171
Soccer	172
Socks.	173
Son	173
Special.	174
Spider	175
Sports	175
Spring	177
Standing/Pulling Up	178
Star	178
Sticker	179
St. Patrick's Day	180
Strawberry	180
Stroller	181
Summer	181
Sun	182
Sunbathing/Sunburn	183
Surfing	184
Swimming	185
Swing	186

T

Talking	187
Teacher/Teaching	189
Teddy Bear	189
Teenager	190
Teeth	191
Telephone	192
Tennis	192
Thanksgiving	192
Tme	193
Toilet/Toilet Training	195

Tongue	196
Toys	196
Tradition	197
Train	198
Treehouse	198
Trouble	199

U

Ultrasound	200
Uncle	200

V

Vacation/Traveling	201
Valentine's Day	203
Volleyball	204
Volunteer	204

W

Walk/Walking	204
War	206
Watermelon	206
Wedding/Marriage	206
Window	208
Women	208
Work	208
World	209
Worm	210
Wreck	210
Wrestling	210

Y

Yard	211
Yard Sale	212
Yell/Yelling	213

Z

Zoo	213

x

TIPS

Suggestions for getting the most out of Top Titles and Tips Too!

1. You know the feeling...you've got the perfect photographs, the perfect papers, the most adorable stickers as well as die cuts, and maybe you've even arranged them on your page. Now, what are going to title your layout? You want that one perfect word or phrase that will catch someone's attention and draw him or her into the pictures and the story on the page; but you're drawing a blank.

   Suppose your layout is of a birthday party. Naturally, the fist topic you would turn to is "birthday." You may be happy with any one of the titles listed here, but you could be missing out on a headline for your page that would sum up the day much better. Look at all possibilities...Was there a theme for the party (example: "bears" or "dolls")? Maybe you want to remember the overwhelming number of "gifts"? If this was your child's first birthday party, you may be surprised to find the title you wanted was listed under "firsts." You may still be most happy with the title you first selected from the birthday list, but to capture the memory, don't limit your options.

2. We've all gone to the scrapbook store with a specific theme in mind and ended up walking out with additional papers and stickers. We didn't know what we would do with them, but we just bought them because they were pretty and we "just had to have them." This book is great for inspiring ideas to use those extra supplies you have on hand. Ask yourself, "What is on the paper?" Flowers? Look up "flowers." This will cross-reference you to "gardening." You don't have to be an avid gardener to find the perfect title here. For example, maybe when you see "Pickin' and Grinnin'", it reminds you of the pictures of your daughter picking flowers for you. This is the beginning of an adorable layout that you may not have otherwise thought of.

   Here is another example of cross-referencing: When you look up "Friends" and "Siblings", you will be cross-referenced to "Multiples." If you gave birth to your children one at a time, you may think those titles would not apply to you.

Initially, these references may not seem relevant to your subject but they are there for a reason. When you check out "Multiples", you may find that a phrase such as "Adorable Duo" or "Triple Trouble" was just what you were searching for.

3. Try pulling different elements out of photos that you want to use but just don't know how. Is it a picture of your "daughter?" Is she surrounded by "toys" or getting into "trouble"? Look up any of these options, or for the best selection, consider the titles listed under all of these topics. Before long, you'll be digging through your patterned paper and die cuts, looking for just the right items to embellish your next scrapbook layout.

4. While looking up topics for the pages or photos that you already have, you'll no doubt stumble across inspiration for layouts that you haven't yet planned. That's always exciting but unfortunately, there may be times when you find yourself in a creative lull. This is the perfect time to scan through the titles in this book. In fact, it's a good idea to do this anyway. By scanning through, you'll notice topics that you did not realize were here or that you wouldn't have thought to look for. There are over 285 topics covered; you won't know what is here unless you look.

5. Design tips are located throughout the book. Use these along with the titles to create one of a kind designs for your pages.

6. A final suggestion. Use all of the blank spaces in the book to your benefit. As you flip through the pages, you may be surprised that a simple phrase may spark so many ideas. Forget what you learned about not writing in books. This is your book now. Use any blank lines or spaces to write down your ideas. We all know how easy it is to forget an idea if we don't write it down the moment we think of it.

Tips to Personalize your Title

A title is one of the most important elements in scrapbooking. Although the pictures are the main focus and the journaling is the most valuable writing on the page, a title is most often the first thing people notice. An intriguing headline is used to entice the reader and make him or her want to know the rest of the story.

As you look through this book, you'll notice some tips to help you personalize your title according to subject. If you've tried these tips as well as the suggestions in the previous sections and you still don't have the title you want for your page, here are more ideas to help you come up with a title of your own:

1. Use each letter of the person's name to start a sentence describing a special characteristic or relationship. We often see this technique done using a single word, but that can be very generic. Instead of writing "Sweet" as the first entry in Skyla's name, it would reveal much more of her personality to write "Says, 'I love my good family' at least once a day."

2. Have the subjects of your photograph handwrite the title themselves, whether it is a child, a friend, or an elderly relative. Someday this may become invaluable to you.

3. Use two or more words that start with the same letter. Try this with your subject's name or a special character trait.

    Example: Chandler the Champion or Rowdy Riley

4. Use a quote overheard at the day's event. Was there something funny that everybody laughed at? If you write it down or use the punchline to title your page, you won't forget it years later. We unfortunately forget a great deal of what we hear.

5. Better yet, is there an expression or favorite saying that your subject often uses? Maybe an appropriate title for a page about your teenager would be "Cool" or "Whatever." This not only shows a little insight to your subject's personality, but it records a memory that will be interesting for generations to come. Wouldn't it tell a lot to future generations to see a page about their Great-Grandmother titled with her favorite saying?

6. Title a page with your subject's nickname. It may be something that everybody calls this person, or it may be a nickname that's exclusively from you. Although you know what the nickname is, other people looking at your album or future generations may not. You may even forget about it years later. If you have a special name you call your baby or young child, use it to title one of the pages in their scrapbook. A nickname is one of the many things that you think you'll remember, but if they outgrow it, you'll likely forget.

7. Modify the name of a favorite movie, television show, book or song.

    Example: Everybody Loves Jayda or Sleepless in Chattanooga.

    If modifying these titles makes them unrecognizable, just use the original title. Years later, this will serve to record your character, taste or culture as it is today.

8. Look beyond the people and tangible items in your photographs. What do you see? What does this picture make you think about? Maybe you see an "Attitude", or you might be reminded of all your special "Memories" with this person. If you don't find the title or topic you are looking for, try simply using that word or phrase as the title.

    Example: ATTITUDE or MEMORIES.

9. If you are still at a loss for words, use the tip above, but add a simple adjective or two in front of your topic.

    Example: My Favorite Toy or A Special Gift.

TITLES

TOP TITLES and TIPS TOO!

adoption

The Greatest Call Ever Answered

How God Brought Us Together

The Best Thing We Ever Did

Do You Believe in Destiny?

My Adoption Story

Together Forever

A New Beginning

A Dream Come True

A Fresh Start

A Labor of Love

The Greatest Gift

The Moment

Destiny

airplane
(see also vacation)

The Wind Beneath My Wings

Braving the Skies

Clear the Runway

TOP TITLES and TIPS TOO!

Up, Up, and Away

Take Flight

Flying High

Flying Ace

Dare to Fly

Super Sonic

Aim High

Soar

---

amusement park

Life is Full of Ups and Downs

What Goes Up Must Come Down

Up and Down, Around and Around

Putting a Spin on Things

Maximum Velocity

An Uplifting Day

Fear Factor

Very Amusing

Away Wheeeeee Go!

A Land of Imagination

Hang On

Wheeeeee!

---

angel

Angels Watching Over Us

Shh...Angel Sleeping

This Is How An Angel Sleeps...

Grandparents are Angels in Disguise

Children are Angels with Crooked Halos

Precious Angel

My Guardian Angel

I'm No Angel

Heaven Sent

The Face of an Angel

A Little Touch of Heaven

For Heaven's Sake

Touched by an Angel

Our Angel

TIP

Pencil your title, then go over each letter with several small consecutive shapes. For example, on a patriotic layout, use several small stars to make up each letter of the title.

TOP TITLES and TIPS TOO!

A Perfect Angel

My Cherub

Heavenly

Animal
(see also specific animals)

Down on the Farm

Party Animal

God's Creatures

Petting Zoo

Critters

Wild Life

Anniversary
(see also Love)

Happy Yesterdays, Happier Tomorrows

Happily Married for 15 Years

Still Going Strong After All These Years

> **TIP**
> Use a quote from your spouse on this day or a line from a special anniversary card.

Then and Now

Through the Years

A Life of Love

Together Forever

So Far, So Good

And They Said It Would Never Last

He's Still My Prince Charming

We've Made It This Far!

Then, Now and Forever

You're Still the One

ANT

No Ifs, Ants, or Bugs About It

Ants in My Pants

apple

An Apple a Day...

The Apple of My Eye

Bushels of Fun

The Apple Doesn't Fall Far from the Tree

School Days

TOP TITLES and TIPS TOO!

As American as Apple Pie

When Life Gives You Apples, Make Applesauce

A is for Apple

One Bad Apple in the Bunch

Sour Apples

Picking-N-Grinning

The Pick of the Crop

Archery

BULLSEYE

Right on Target

Sharpshooter

Straight as an Arrow

Armed Forces

(see Military)

Art

(see also color/coloring)

Art from the Heart

Doodle Bug

Express Yourself

Use Your Imagination

Allow Yourself to Imagine

Look What I Did

A Work of Art

A Real Piece of Work

Beauty is in the Eye of the Beholder

Masterpiece

Imagination

The Next Picasso

ATTITUDE

I'm in Charge Here

This Is How It's Gonna Be...

Warning: Attitude in Use

Where There's a Will, There's a Way

That's Mister Sean to You!

I'm the BOSS

COCKY

SASSY

I'm Too Cute for Words

Big Shot

The Divine Divas

DIVA

AUNT

Being an Aunt Means…

World's Best Aunt

Aunt Awesome

My Friend, My Aunt

Aunt I Sweet?

It's All Relative

My Aunt Rules!

AUTUMN

(see FALL)

TIP

When using punched or die cut letters, use themed stickers for the "holes" of the letters.

TOP TITLES and TIPS TOO!

BABY

(see also BOY, CHILD and GIRL)

Love at First Sight

New Life, New Love

Oh, Baby!

A Gift From Above

Our Bundle From Heaven

The Greatest Miracle of All

Make a Wish...

Introducing...

It's a Small, Small World

Our Perfect Angel

Our Baby Angel

I Wish for You...

My Promise to You...

Birth Day

Baby Me

Welcome

American Made

Innocence

Heads Up

Our New Arrival

TOP TITLES and TIPS TOO!

A Labor of Love

A Star is Born

I Have Arrived

PERFECTION

Introducing the World's Most Beautiful Baby

It's a Boy!

It's a Girl!

The Love of Our Lives

You've Got the Cutest Little Baby Face

A Bundle of Joy

Lying in the Lap of Luxury

Big Things Come in Small Packages

Our Dream Come True

God's Greatest Gift

An Answered Prayer

Our Special Delivery

A Lullaby Moment

Ten Tiny Toes

A Button Nose, Cherry Lips and Ten Tiny Toes

Baking

FLOUR POWER

Cutie Pie

Let 'em Eat Cake

Clear the Runway

TOP TITLES and TIPS TOO!

I'll Have My Cake and Eat It Too

From the Kitchen of Paula

(put your title on a die cut label or make a recipe card)

As American as Apple Pie

Sugar and Spice and Everything Nice

SWEET TOOTH

What's Cooking, Good Looking?

Decorated with Love

Loving You is as Easy as Pie

Batter Up!

Cookie Monsters

Ball

(see also Sports and specific games)

Havin' a Ball

Play Ball!

ALL-STAR

On the Ball

Baptism/Christening/Church

A Blessing

A Child of God

TOP TITLES and TIPS TOO!

Our Child of God

Soul Survivor

For Heaven's Sake

New & Improved

Amazing Grace

Bless This Child

Our Sunday Best

Our Sundae Best (use those ice cream stickers!)

Soul Searching

Have Faith

Count Your Blessings

A Day of Rest

A Day of Grace

A Life Altared

Amen

Sunday's Child is Full of Grace

Baseball

(see also Sports)

Lil' Slugger

Our Little Slugger

HOMERUN

Take Me Out to the Ball Game

The Home Stretch

TOP TITLES and TIPS TOO!

Who's on First?

Batter Up!

Playing the Field

Major League Trainee

Rookie

Spring into Action

ALL-STAR

All-Star in Training

Havin' a Ball

Play Ball

Major Leagues, Here I Come

Hit and Run

Seventh-Inning Stretch

BasketBall

(see also sports)

WHOOSH!

Nothing But Net

King of the Court

HOOPla

BIG SHOT

HOT SHOT

Hoop Dreams

NBA Trainee

TOP TITLES and TIPS TOO!

Laying Bricks

He Shoots! He Scores!

MVP

MVP in Training

BATHTIME

(see also BUBBLEBATH/BUBBLES)

H2Oh!

Luv the Tub

Good Clean Fun

Squeaky Clean

Soap Opera

Rub a Dub in a Tub

Just Add Water

Makin' Waves

Get Wet

Waterbug

A Day at the Spa

You Quack Me Up!

Water, Water Everywhere

A Splashing Good Time

Water Whimsy

Tubs of Fun

Tub Scrubbin'

TOP TITLES and TIPS TOO!

Tub Time

Rub a Dub Dub, Two Boys in a Tub

All Washed Up

Wet-n-Wild

Bathing Beauty

Did You Say "Bathtime" or "Playtime"?

SPLISH SPLASH

Beach

Beach Bum

The Prince and His Sand Castle

A Princess and Her Castle

Beach Babes

Beach Babies

Makin' Waves

Water, Water Everywhere

Sand Man

Little Mermaid

TIP
On beach vacations, write the location and date in the sand and have each person write his or her own name. A zoom shot of this family memory can serve as the title of your page.

TOP TITLES and TIPS TOO!

Don't Be Afraid to Get Your Feet Wet

Sun, Sea, Sand & Shells

Oceanography

A Whale of a Good Time

A Fantasea Vacation

Sand-wich anyone?

Beach Buddies

You, Me and the Deep Blue Sea

A Wave of Excitement

At Sea

From Sea to Shining Sea

Sunsationally Sandtastic!

Three by the Sea

A Seaside Adventure

Beach Party

The Beauty and the Beach

Happy as a Clam

Getting Wave Reviews

Catch a Wave

A Beautiful Day for the Beach

The Sands of Time

Feelin' Crabby

Down by the Sea Shore

Jewels of the Sea

A Seashell Search on the Seashore

H2Oh!

Beauty

Beauty, Joy, Grace…Brittany

Radiance

A Perfect 10

Beauty Gives Joy

Good Looks Run in the Family

As Pretty as a Picture

As Pretty as a Picture of Amber

Bee

Bee-ootiful

To Bee or Not to Bee

Lil' Honeybee

The Queen Bee

Beecause I Love You

Beeing Cute

Cute as Can Bee

Catching a Buzz

Bee Sweet

TOP TITLES and TIPS TOO!

Sweet as Honey

Hi, Honey!

Buzz Off!

Bicycle

(see also Firsts)

Try-cycle

Easy Rider

If at First You Don't Succeed...

Try, Try Again

PEDDLER

Happy Trails

Peddle Pushin'

The Path Taken

Biker Boy

Head for the Hills

Trail Mix

Hot on the Trail

Balancing Act

Practice Makes Perfect

Backyard Bike-a-thon

Have Some Balance in Your Life

Steady...Steady...

I'm Two Tired

Trial and Error

Trail and Error

Hittin' the Trail

Trail Blazers

Steering Clear

Stop-N-Go

Birds

Birds of a Feather Flock Together

A Little Bird Told Me...

This is for the Birds

The Wind Beneath My Wings

Spread Your Wings

Feathered Friends

Flights of Fancy

Up, Up, and Away

Home Tweet Home

Lovebirds

Songbird

Dare to Fly

Take Flight

Soar

TOP TITLES and TIPS TOO!

Tweet Tweet

As Free as a Bird

The Early Bird Gets the Worm

As Light As A Feather

Backyard Beauty

Jailbird

BiRTHDay

(see also Party and specific Themes)

It's the Big ONE

Bear-ly 2 Years Old

Look at Me! I'm 3!

More and More Cute at 4

Four No More!

Five Alive

Bye-Bye 5

7 is Heaven

8 is Great

Fine at 9

Double Digits!

TiP

For a child's page, write some of the letters backwards, or purposely misspell a word or two.

11 is Heaven

Just BeTWEEN Us, I'm 12

You're HOW OLD?

Aged to Perfection

The Age of Innocence

Forever Young

An Ageless Wonder

Birthday Wishes

I Wish…

An Oldie but Goodie

Make a Wish

SURPRISE!

I'll Have My Cake and Eat It Too

Let's Party!

With Age Comes Wisdom

Still Young at Heart

BLOCKS

The Cute Kid on the Block

The New Blocks on the Kid

Blockhead

Block Party!

Boat/Cruise

Row, Row, Row Your Boat

The Captain of My Heart

The Anchor of My Soul

Go Overboard

Sink or Swim

Water World

Captain Mathew

Makin' Waves

Love Boat

A Real Lifesaver

Water, Water Everywhere

Bon Voyage

Shipping and Handling

Cruisin'

My Ship Has Finally Come In

Anchors Away

Ahoy, Matey

Ships Ahoy

Sail Away

TOP TITLES and TIPS TOO!

BOOK

Bedtime Story

Bookworm

A Novel Idea

Hittin' the Books

A Real Page Turner

Future Librarian

And the Story Begins...

Cover to Cover

Never Judge a Book by its Cover

Playing by the Book

Allow Yourself to Imagine

STORYTIME

An Open Book

An Open Book Opens Minds

TIP

Try using the title and theme from a favorite book. Another suggestion: Title this page with a phrase your child uses when asking you to read.
Example: "Read Me, Mommy."

TOP TITLES and TIPS TOO!

BOWLING

Pin Bustin'

No Time to Spare

That's Right Up My Alley

SuperBowl

Life is a BOWL of Cherries

You Bowl Me Over

BOXING

(see FIGHT/FIGHTING)

BOY/BOYS

(see also son)

Boys Will Be Boys

No Girls Allowed

It's a Guy Thing

Pure Boy

All Boy

The Boys of Summer

Bouncing Baby Boy

Boy, Oh Boy!

TOP TITLES and TIPS TOO!

Brotherly Love

Rugged Good Looks

What a Guy!

My Boy, My Joy

So Handsome

Tough Guy

Little Man

Busy Boy

Prince Charming

Prince Charming in Training

Thank Heaven for Little Boys

Boys Rule, Girls Drool

Backyard Boys

Boys Club

Boy Wonder

Snakes and Snails and Puppy Dog Tails

Rough and Tumble

Boyfriend

(see also Date and Love)

My One and Only

Mr. Right Now

Boy, Oh Boyfriend!

TOP TITLES and TIPS TOO!

CRUSH

Puppy Love

Boy Meets Girl

A True Romantic

Opposites Attract

Cute Couple

Beauty and the Beast

So Far, So Good

BOY SCOUTS

Scout's Honor

Always Prepared

Be Prepared for Anything

On My Honor

Scout It Out

Break-up

New Beginnings

Love Hurts

Divorce Court

Out With the Old, In With the New

Can I Pick 'Em or What?

What Was I Thinking?

Playing Solitaire

Dismissed

Split (use a torn picture)

Letting Go

Give Me a Break

Time Heals

She Loves Me, She Loves Me Not

A Change of Heart

Good Riddance

C-YA!

See Ya' Around

A Good Man is Hard to Find

The End.

Brother
(see also Boys, Family and Sibling)

My Brother, My Friend

A Brother's Love

A Brother is a Lifelong Friend

What is a Big Brother For?

My Brother's Keeper

TOP TITLES and TIPS TOO!

I'm the Little Brother

Band of Brothers

Oh, Brother…

Friends from the Start

A Brother Understands

Brothers Since the Beginning, Friends 'Til the End

Big Brother's Watching Over You

BUBBLEBATH/BUBBLES

(see also BATH)

Bubble Trouble

A Bubbly Personality

Bubble-ing Over With Fun

Bubble-ing Over With Laughter

Double the Bubbles, Double the Fun

DOUBLY BOUBLY

TIP

Take a tightly zoomed photo of a prominent sign at your event. Try taking several shots, zooming in on only a few letters at a time, then cutting the letters out and pasting them on cardstock the color of the original sign.

Yummy Bubble Gummy

Blowing Bubbles

Bubble Babe

Bubble Buds

SUDZ

Bubble Butt

BUBBLE BUBBLE BUBBLE

Bug

CREEPY CRAWLY

BUG OFF

Cute as a Bug

As Snug as a Bug in a Rug

No Ifs, Ants, or Bugs About It

June Bugs

The Jitter Bug

Caught a Bug (this is cute for a "sick" page)

Bug Catcher

Cootie Bug

Quit Bugging Me

Love Bug

Bit by the Love Bug

Fashion Bug

SHUTTERBUG

Computer Bug

BUS

The Wheels on the Bus Go 'Round and 'Round

Risky BUSiness

A Bus for Us

Bus Stop, Bus Go

Bus Boy

BUTTERFLY

Butterfly Kisses

Flights of Fancy

Flutterby

Grace

Dare to Fly

Up, Up & Away

A Dance of Grace

The Wind Beneath My Wings

FLITTER FLITTER

Spread Your Wings

My Heart's A-Flutter

As Beautiful as a Butterfly

As Gentle as a Butterfly

Butterfly Beauty

Backyard Beauty

Well, Flitter

cake

(see also Baking)

Let 'em Eat Cake

I'll Have My Cake and Eat It Too

SWEET TOOTH

---

camping

Happy Campers

S'More Good Times

Our Neck of the Woods

What Was That Noise?

Roughing It Easy

Wood You Like To Go Camping?

Did You Hear That?

Campfire Fun

Unplugged

Home Sweet Motorhome

Under the Stars

The Great Outdoors

Roughin' It

Candy/Chocolate

So Much Candy, So Little Time

SWEETHEART

SWEET TOOTH

Sweets for a Sweetie

Sweet, Like Skyla

CANDYLAND

Give Me Some Sugar, Baby

Eat Now, Diet Later

Chocaholic

Spoil Yourself

Dandy Candy

INDULGE

A Basic Necessity of Life

Treat Yourself

Sweet Dreams

Sweet Nothings

car
(see also Driving and vacation)

A Classic

Vroom Vroom

Driving Us Crazy

The Pit Crew

The Wheel Deal

Built for Speed

carousel

Up and Down, 'Round and 'Round

MERRY-Go-Round

Beauty in Motion

TIP
When using a die cut machine to create your title, cut each letter out using a solid color as well as a themed patterned paper. Use the patterned letters as a shadow for the solid ones.

Cat

(see also Pet)

Copy Cat

Cat-titude

Cats Are People Too

Here Kitty, Kitty!

Scaredy Cat

Ryan and Me-ow

Kool Kitty

Good Kitty

PURRfect

M-E-O-W

Sadie is the Cat's Meow

One Cool Cat

The Dog Did It!

The Nine Lives of Fluffy

Fancy Feline

Look What the Cat Dragged In

Playful as a Kitten

Crazy Cat

CHALK

(see also ART and COLOR/COLORING)

CHALK TALK

Chalk One Up for Nathan

Let's Chalk About It

CHEERLEADER

Go! Fight! Win!

We've Got Spirit, Yes We Do…

Team Leaders

Short Skirts and Attitudes

Pom Pom Girls

Team Spirit

School Spirit

RALLY

TIP

Use a line from a popular or favorite chant. Even if it's one that you're so tired of hearing, and it makes YOU want to scream, this could be the one that brings back the most memories in the future.

Cherry

Life is a Bowl of Cherries

Cheery Cherries

I Love You Cherry Much

I Love You With a Cherry On Top

I Cherryish You

Cherry Lips

Chicken

Slick Chick

One Sick Chick

Cock-a-Doodle-Doo

C-O-C-K-Y

Chick This Out!

Tip
Look at the titles listed under "photography." These can be used for many general photographs.

CHILD/CHILDREN

(see also Baby, Boy, Girl and Cute)

As Good as Gold

A Child is God's Greatest Gift

My Inspiration

Kiddin' Around

Lil' Explorer

My Heart & Soul

Priceless

Wit & Wisdom from a 7-year old

Thank God

This Child of Mine

Leave It to Spencer

Kids will be Kids

The Key to Happiness

My Wish for You…

Unconditional Love

TNT (Tough & Tender)

These are a Few of My Favorite Things

The More the Merrier

My Heaven on Earth

Count Your Blessings

Wild Child

Innocence

The Age of Innocence

TOP TITLES and TIPS TOO!

What Matters Most

Spoiled Rotten

The Essence of Jacalyn

Child's Play

The World's Best Kid

Kool Kid

Children Make the World a Happier Place

Our Pride and Joy

A Child of All Seasons

Children Put the Magic in Life

A Child Enjoys Life's Simple Pleasures

Everyday Moments are Cherished Moments

Children are Angels with Crooked Halos

Christmas
(see also Gifts and Santa Claus)

Christmas Princess

A Christmas Prince

Holidaze

O' Christmas Tree

You Make Me Very Merry

From Our Family to Yours

You're So Deer

A Christmas Story

O' Holy Night

All I Want for Christmas is…

Christmas Magic

Holiday Memories

Scrooge

Our Little Elves

Santa's Helper

All Hearts Come Home for Christmas

I'll Be Home For Christmas

'Tis the Season for Love

Home for the Holidays

Children Put the Magic in Christmas

'Twas the Night Before Christmas

Our Christmas Angel

As Stuffed as the Christmas Stockings

TRADITION

Christmas Cousins

A Holly, Jolly Christmas

Naughty or Nice

Trimming the Tree

Joy to the World

Wish List

Jolly Holidays

TOP TITLES and TIPS TOO!

So Many Toys, So Little Time

Toys, Toys, Everywhere

circle

My Circle of Friends

Round 'em Up

Coming Full Circle

circus

The Big Top

The Greatest Show on Earth

Lions, Tigers, and Bears...Oh, My!

Clowning Around

Side Show

Circus Freaks

clothing

(see dress-up)

TOP TITLES and TIPS TOO!

CLOUDS
(see also Heaven and Rain)

Heaven Sent

Every Cloud Has a Silver Lining

Our Bundle From Heaven

CLOWN

So Silly

Clownin' Around

COLLEGE
(see also Graduation and School)

College Bound

My Dorm Away from Home

Dorm Sweet Dorm

College or Bust

College Knowledge

TIP
Title this page with your school's name, initials, mascot, or motto.

• 41 •

TOP TITLES and TIPS TOO!

Kollege, Here I Come!

Free at Last

Far from Home

To the First Degree

---

color/coloring

(see also art)

Color Me Silly

The Many Colors of Trista

Pretty with Pink

A Splash of Color

A Colorful Personality

Color Coordinated

Color My World

Showing My True Colors

Pretty Scribbles

Scribble Scribble Scribble

Doodle-ing

VIVID!

---

computer

World Wide Web

The Wild, Wild Web

NETWORKING

Little Computer Bug

I'm Only a Click Away

Get Connected

Connecting...

You've Got Mail

High-Tech Red-Neck

construction

(see also do-it-yourself)

DIG IT

Destruction Zone

Under Destruction

Caution: Boys at Play

Caution: Child at Play

Constructive Play

Dig In!

I Dig Big Trucks

Construction Area

Cooking

(see also Baking)

We're Cookin' Now

What's Cookin', Good Lookin'?

Look What's Cooking

The Kitchen is the Heart of the Home

What's for Dinner?

Seasoned With Love

The Spice of Life

Hail to the Chef

Kiss the Cook

Savory

The Taste Test

Special Recipe

The Secret Ingredient

(Did your child sneeze or scratch his head while helping in the kitchen? This will be funny later.)

The Best You've Ever Tasted

A Well-Seasoned Cook

Chef Keith

Season to Taste

COOKOUT

Boy Meets Grill

Backyard Burgers

Backyard Bash

The Grill of Your Life

Get Grilling

Get Fired Up

A Family Tradition

Me, You & Barbeque

Master of the Grill

COUNTRY

(see also Farm)

The Heart of the Country

Wide Open Spaces

A Little Bit Country

Country Livin'

Country Charm

Hey, Ya'll!

Howdy

Field of Dreams

TOP TITLES and TIPS TOO!

Yee-Haw!

Down on the Farm

cousin
(see also family)

World's Cutest Cousins

I Love You Just Becousin

Being a Cousin Means...

Kissing Cousins

Christmas Cousins

My Cousin, My Friend

cow

Lil' Cowpoke

Udderly Adorable

That's No Bull

Holy Cow!

Got Milk?

TIP
Use vellum paper to trace letters from a book or magazine.

Milkin' It For All It's Worth

You MOOve Me

HOWDY!

COWBOY

Giddy Up!

Lil' Cowpoke

Howdy, Pardner

A Rootin' Tootin' Good Time

My Heroes Have Always Been Cowboys

There's a New Sheriff in Town

Honky Tonkin'

Cowgirl Wanted

Go West

Rodeo

HOWDY!

Round 'em Up

WANTED

$10,000 REWARD

The Best in the West

Stick 'em Up!

The Wild, Wild West

Horsin' Around

Buckaroo

Yee-Haw!

crafts
(see also sewing)

Handmade with Love

A Personal Touch

Homemade Memories

How Adorable

C-R-A-F-T-Y

A Gift from the Heart

Look What I Made

crawling
(see also firsts)

Look Out World, Here I Come!

Going, Going, Gone

I Think I Can, I Think I Can, I Can!

The Little Engine that Could

Practice Makes Perfect

Baby in Motion

On the Move

Staying Grounded

Lil' Explorer

Bottoms Up!

On the Go

Get a Move On, Baby!

Ready for Action

Get Moving

Creepy Crawly

crocodile

Crocodile Tears

See Ya' Later, Alligator

Afterwhile, Crocodile

crying

(see also sad)

Cry Baby

Don't Cry, Baby

Crocodile Tears

TOP TITLES and TIPS TOO!

It's Just an Expression

For Cryin' Out Loud

A Crying Shame

I Laughed. I Cried.

Hush-a-bye, Baby

Gloom & Doom

Growing Pains

CUT
(see also injury)

On the Cutting Edge

Cuttin' Up

Cut It Out

A Cut Above the Rest

CUTE
(see also Beauty)

Cute as a Button

Just as Cute as I Can Be

Cute-N-Cuddly

Cutie Pie

Little Charmer

Prince Charming

Personality Plus

Absolutely Adorable

Too Cute For Words

You've Got the Cutest Lil' Baby Face

Cute Couple

Cute is My Middle Name

I Couldn't be More Lovable if I Tried

Rugged Good Looks

ICURAQT

So Handsome

Pure Perfection

Cute Kid

Daddy
(see Father)

TOP TITLES and TIPS TOO!

Dance
(see also Music)

Dance the Night Away

Dancing Duo

Let Your Heart Dance

Kick Up Your Heels

The Belle of the Ball

RadioActive

Shall We Dance?

The Entertainer

Two Left Feet

Twinkle Toes

SIDEKICKS

Tiny Dancer

The Baby Boogie

Dancin' to a Different Beat

Date
(see also Boyfriend and Girlfriend)

Cute Couple

Romance

Date Night

Boy Meets Girl

Variety is the Spice of Life

The Dating Game

Cherish the Moment

A Night on the Town

I Thought He'd Never Ask

How Did It Get So Late, So Early?

DREAM DATE

Daughter
(see also Baby, Child and Girl)

A Daughter is a Reflection of Her Mother's Heart

A Daughter is a Mother's Best Friend

Like Mother, Like Daughter

Lifelong Friend and Daughter

She's Our Heart and Soul

A Daughter is Heaven on Earth

A Daughter is Love

Death
(see also Memories)

Gone But Not Forgotten

An Angel Watches Over Us

TOP TITLES and TIPS TOO!

Rest Peacefully

In Loving Memory

Keeping the Memory Alive

Unforgettable

I'll Love You Forever

We Miss You

Cherish the Memory

Sorrowful Day

Always Loved, Never Forgotten

My Guardian Angel

Diet

Light and Fluffy

Go Figure!

Loser!

Weighting Anxiously

Weigh To Go!

Here's the Skinny...

The Incredible Shrinking Woman

Waist Not, Want Not

Eat Now, Diet Later

Through Thick or Thin

Fit and Fabulous

Slim and Trim

Living Large

Think Thin

Light as a Feather

Dinosaur

DINOmite!

Prehistoric Fun

Dirty/Messy

A Little Dirt Never Hurt Anybody

This Little Piggy

Muddy Buddies

Mud Buds

Lil' Pig

YUCK!

Pig Sty

What's a Little Mud Between Two Friends?

Getting Down and Dirty

What a Mess

Trashed

Look What I Did

I'm a Mess

Could Somebody Call a Janitor?

Have You Ever Seen Such a Mess?

Uh-Oh!

Oops!

Divorce

(See Break-up)

Doctor

(see also illness and injury)

This Won't Hurt a Bit

This Hurts Me More Than it Hurts You

Is There a Doctor in the House?

Say, "Ahhh"

Miracle Cure

TIP

Diagnose your subject. Example: Diagnosis: Touchmenotitis.

FIRST AID

Nevermind, I'm Suddenly Feeling Better

Dr. SCARY

Nurse Starla

Dr. Trent

Diagnosis: Spoiledrottenitis

Diagnosis: Homesick

Diagnosis: Lovesick

A Clean Bill of Health

A Picture of Health

What's Up, Doc?

All Better

DOG

(see also PET)

Snakes and Snails and Puppy Dog Tails...

Puppy Love

A Boy's Best Friend

Hot Diggity-Dog!

Pampered Pooch

Dog Days of Summer

I Woof You

Good Dog

TOP TITLES and TIPS TOO!

One Howl of a Dog

It's a Dog's Life

Doggone Adorable

Make No Bones About It...I'm Cute!

Take a Bow-Wow

Puppy Play

Do-it-yourself/Remodeling
(see also construction)

If I Build It, They Will Come

If I Build It, They Will Use It

Can I Build It? Yes! I Can!

A Jack of All Trades

A Work in Progress

Rome Wasn't Built in a Day

Raise the Roof

Room for Improvement

Do-it-herself

Power Project

Before(the headache) & After(the headache)

Some Assembly Required

Fixer Upper

Room to Breathe

From Start to Finish

TOP TITLES and TIPS TOO!

What a Difference

Great Expectations

Home Improvement

Caution: Men at Work

Caution: Perrys at Work

Caution: Husband at Work

All Decked Out

From House to Dream Home

Mr. Fix-it

Tool Time

DOLL

(see also Baby)

All Dolled Up

Living Dolls

My Baby & Me

Oh, What a Doll!

Mommy in Training

Dreams

If You Can Dream It, You Can Be It

Conceive It. Believe It. Achieve It.

The Path Taken

The Path Not Taken

What If...

Daydreams Fulfilled

Reach for the Stars

Spread Your Wings & Fly

Follow Your Rainbow

The Prince of Dreams

Dress-Up/Style
(see also Fairytale)

All Dressed Up - Where Can We Go?

All Dressed Up with No Place to Go

You've Got Style, Baby

Dressed for Success

Steppin' Out in Style

Girly Girl

Under Wraps

Best Dressed

Worst Dressed

A Real Character

Girls Will be Girls

Clothes Call!

TOP TITLES and TIPS TOO!

The Belle of the Ball

Dress-up Days

Fashion(un)able

All Dolled Up

It's All in the Accessories, Darling

Role "Model"

A "Model" Member of Society

Hot Stuff

Glamour Girl

Cover Girl

Best Dressed

Accessorize, Accessorize, Accessorize

How Do I Look?

Lookin' Good

How Do You Like Me Now?

Driving
(see also Car, Race and Wreck)

On the Road Again

Road Warrior

The Road to Discovery

Driver's Ed…Teacher: Dad

Road Crew

TOP TITLES and TIPS TOO!

I'm in the Driver's Seat Now

Yield

Stop-N-Go

Begin Your Journey

Driving Me Crazy

Are We There Yet?

The Grand Prix

Speed Racer

Going the Extra Mile

How Much Longer?

Steering Clear

No Direction in Life

Two Wrong Turns Don't Make a Right

Caution: Teenager Behind the Wheel

Along for the Ride

Hang On

The Ride of My Life

TIP
Vary the idea of title blocks, using shapes other than the usual square.

Drums
(see also Music)

Lil' Drummer Boy

BANG! CLASH! BANG!

The Beat of a Different Drummer

Ears

Have You Heard?

Say What?

I'm All Ears

The Ear-ly Years

Lend Me Your Ears

Huh?

Earth
(see World)

Easter

An Egg-stra Special Easter

Hoppy Easter

There's Nobunny Like You

He is Risen

Keep Your Eye on the Prize

The Thrill of the Hunt

Chick This Out!

The Hunt Is On

Everybunny Loves Me

Easter Parade

Somebunny Special

Hopping Down the Bunny Trail

Hippity!Hoppity!Happy Easter!

Don't Put All Your Eggs In One Basket

Eggstatic!

Egg-specially Cute

An Egg-stra Big Mess

Simply to Dye For!

TIP

For your title, substitute die cuts or stickers in place of some of the words.

Eggsposed!

Egg Art

Scrambling for Eggs

Eating

(see also Messy)

Mmm!Mmm!Good!

YUMMY

All I Want to Do is Chew Chew Chew

MUNCHTIME

Eating Again?

The Princess and the Peas

Eat Now, Diet Later

I Love You Alunch

Let's Eat

Lunch Munch

Eat, Drink, and Be Merry

Life is a Bowl of Cereal

Cereal Killer

Bite Bite

Table Scraps

TOP TITLES and TIPS TOO!

Comfort Food (use those sleeping pictures)

Kid Kuisine

The Taste Test

Food for Thought

You Can Dish It Out but You Can't Take It

Food Foolery

Watch What You Eat

You Are What You Eat

She's Gonna Blow!

Phhtttthh!

Taste Buds

Going…Going…Gone!

Absolutely, Positively Scrumptious

A Taste of Things to Come

Come 'N Get It!

You Bowl Me Over

Seconds, please

The Lunch Bunch

I'm Stuffed!

It's a Matter of Taste

What's Cookin', Good Lookin'?

TOP TITLES and TIPS TOO!

Engagement

YES

I said, "Yes"

I Thought You Would Never Ask

Will You Marry Me?

I Found My Prince

The Big Question

An Engaging Evening

Romance

Can I Pick 'Em or What?

The Wedding Planner

Bride-to-be

Diamonds are a Girl's Best Friend

ENGAGED

Breathtaking

This Magic Moment

Always and Forever

Engaged at Last

The Future Mr. & Mrs.

TIP
Use a quote from this special day.

TOP TITLES and TIPS TOO!

Exercise

Eat Now, Exercise Later

Burnin' Calories

No Pain, No Gain

The Way I See it is…No Pain, No Pain

HUFF HUFF HUFF

…and Breathe, 2, 3, 4…

Feeling Fit

Fit and Firm

HARDBODY

Hardbody in Training

Feel the Burn

Go Figure!

BUFF

Pumped Up

Huffin' and Puffin'

Be Strong

Firm, Fit, and Fabulous

Everyday Life

A Day in the Life of Abbey

Just Another Day

Just Another Day at the Perry House

The Journey of Life

Treasured Days

Everyday Life

Being Me...

Day by Day

Cherish these Days

The Simple Life

Homemade Memories

A Typical Day

These are the Days to Remember

Days are Fleeting, Memories are Forever

The Magic of Everyday

Eyes

(see also glasses)

The Window to the Soul

For Your Eyes Only

Look on the Bright Side

Seeing Eye to Eye

Baby Blues

Out of Sight!

A Sight to Behold

What a Sight to See!

Love at First Sight

TOP TITLES and TIPS TOO!

Keeping an Eye on Things

Have You Seen Candace?

SPARKLE

So Much to See

Reflections

I Spy

Peek-a-boo!

I See You!

Peepers

Brown-eyed Beauty

Blue-eyed Beauty

A Heaven of Hazel

The Beauty of the World

Do You See What I See?

Optical Illusion

Eye See You

Fairytale

(see also Dress-up)

Once Upon a Time...

As You Wish...

Her Majesty

The King and His Castle

A Magical Fantasy

Mystical Wonder

Pretty Pixie

The Belle of the Ball

Imagination Gives You Wings

Waiting for My Prince

Queen for a Day

Our Little Prince

Our Princess

My Knight in Shining Armor

The Royal Jester

ROYALTY

Hear Ye, Hear Ye...

Use Your Imagination

I Believe...

Daydream Believer

...Happily Ever After

Fall

(see also Pumpkin)

Harvest Time

Harvest Happiness

TOP TITLES and TIPS TOO!

Pumpkin' Patch

Turning Over a New Leaf

On a Crisp Autumn Day...

The Cool Crisp Days of Autumn

Fall Into Fun

The Fall Guy

Piles of Smiles

A Child of All Seasons

A Crisp Breeze and Crunchy Leaves

Everything is Falling into Place

The Essence of Fall

Fall-ing in Love

Fall Fling

I'm Falling for You

Golden Days

Awesome Autumn

Pile on the Fun!

A Sign of the Season

It's Fall, Ya'll

TIP

After choosing your title, look at the letters and decide if a themed sticker can easily replace any of the letters. For example, baseball bats can be substituted for the letter "I" on a sports layout.

Having a Hay Day

Hay, There!

Family

Family Matters

A Family Affair

The Ties that Bind the Family Together

My Life, My Love, My Family, My World

All in the Family

A Family that Prays Together Stays Together

A Family that Plays Together Stays Together

One Big Happy Family

Family Portrait

Family Fun

The Gangs All Here

The Heart of the Home

It's All Relative

Ancestrally Challenged

Our Legacy

The Pell Legacy

GENERATIONS

We Begin and End With Family

Family Values

Obviously, Good Looks Run in the Family

Family Tree
(see also Family and Heritage)

Branching Out

Our Tree has Grown a Few Nuts

Past, Present and Our Future

Remember Your Roots

"Leave" Your Mark

Turning Over a New Leaf

Farm
(see also Country)

Family Farm Fun

Lil' Farmer

Lil' Farmer Logan

Down on the Farm

Hay, There!

Having a Hay Day

TOP TITLES and TIPS TOO!

FATHER

My Hero

Like Father, Like Son

Like Daddy, Like Daughter

Daddy's Girl

Daddy's Little Helper

My Heart Belongs to Daddy

My First Love

Do Dad

(list what Daddy "does" or what Daddy and the kids do together)

I Owe It All To You

A Super Man

A Dad of All Trades

A Father's Love

Guidance

Daddy's Day

In Dad We Trust

The "Lap" of Luxury

Strong Man, Gentle Heart

TIP
When using title blocks, layer a solid color block on a patterned block, overlapping only slightly for a subtle composition.

TOP TITLES and TIPS TOO!

A Living Legacy

Head Honcho

Father Knows Best

The King

Being a Daddy Means…

Father-in-Law

My Other Father

Father by Marriage

His Father, My Friend

Feet

Put Your Best Foot Forward

Kick Up Your Heels

Nothing More Sweet Than the Patter of Little Feet

Pitter Patter

Ten Tiny Toes

Barefoot and Fancy Free

Footloose and Fancy Free

These Feet were Made for Walking

Tiny Tootsies

Barefootin'

A Perfect 10

Heart & Sole

2 Left Feet

Stinky Feet

You Knock My Socks Off

This Little Piggy...

The Agony of Defeet

Shoo!

Step-by-Step

Step by Tiny Step

FiGHT/FiGHTiNG

Down for the Count

A Real Knockout

Puttin' Up a Fight

Allies at War

Tough Enough?

The Fist of Fury

Invincible

Put 'em Up!

Keep Your Eye on the Prize

A Knock-down Drag-out

Rough and Tumble

Fight Night

A Fight 'Til the End

Fire

Jumping Out of the Frying Pan, Into the Fire

HOT HOT HOT

Up in Flames

Where's the Fire?

Don't Play With Fire

The Heat Is On

A Blaze of Glory

Things are Heating Up

Feel the Burn

Too Hot to Handle

Sound the Alarm

Hot Stuff

Fire!!!

Where There's Smoke, There's Fire

TOP TITLES and TIPS TOO!

Firsts

There's a First Time for Everything

Life is Full of Firsts

The First Time Around

I Think I Can, I Think I Can, I Can!

The Little Engine that Could

Look What I Can Do!

Practice Makes Perfect

First Thing's First

Just Learning

Rookie

If at First You Don't Succeed…

Milestone

What an Effort!

I Did It!

I'll Do Anything Once

Fish/Fishing

The Catch of the Day

There's Something Fishy Going On Here

Fishing for Compliments

I'm a Keeper

TOP TITLES and TIPS TOO!

Gone Fishin' (Again)

Look What I Caught

Eat, Sleep, Fish

A Reel-y Good Time

I'm Hooked

Nice Catch!

The Catch of My Life

The Reel Deal

Hook, Line & Sinker

FLOWER

(see also gardening)

Love in Bloom

Blooming Idiots

Friendship in Bloom

Memory is the Power to Gather Roses in the Winter

Flower Power

Spring Has Sprung

Growing Like a Weed

A Rose by Any Other Name Smells Just as Sweet

Stop and Smell the Roses

April Showers Bring May Flowers

Backyard Beauty

An Annual Event

A Perennial Favorite

Sow Seeds of Kindness

He Loves Me, He Loves Me Not

Freshly Picked with You in Mind

Hand-painted by Angels

Flower Girl

Tiptoe Through the Tulips

Paradise

The Best of Buds

Buds

Can I Pick 'Em or What?

Oh, How They Grow!

Let Love Bloom

A Bouquet of Fun

Beautiful Two-lips

A Green Thumb

I Try. They Die.

Bloom & Gloom

Garden Party

Take Time to Smell the Flowers

Life is Rosy

Lattice Have Fun

TOP TITLES and TIPS TOO!

Blossom

A Budding Romance

FOOTBALL
(see also SPORTS)

Touchdown!

MVP

MVP in Training

NFL Trainee

Playing the Field

FRIEND
(see also MULTIPLES)

Bestest Buddies

The Best of Friends, The Best of Times

2 Peas In A Pod

TIP
For sports layouts, use a catch phrase from your favorite team or game announcer. Example: "It's Football Time in Tennessee!"

TOP TITLES and TIPS TOO!

Two of a Kind

Friendship in Bloom

My Circle of Friends, Let It Never Be Broken

To Know Him is to Love Him

What are Friends for?

The Gang

Inseparable

Partners in Crime

PlayMates

Like Family

The More the Merrier

Friends 'Til the End

Two's Company

Three's Company

Friends Forever

Friends Through Thick or Thin

Me and My Shadow

Friends in Sunshine and in Shade

Sidekicks

Love One Another

Gossip Gossip Gossip

Frog

Ribbit Ribbit

Don't Worry, Be Hoppy

It Ain't Easy Being Green

Kiss Me…

I May Be A Prince, You Never Know

Is This Leap Year?

Feelin' Froggy? Jump!

Toadally Awesome

Four-Wheeling

Trail Blazer

Hittin' the Trail

Trail & Error

Happy Trails

Free Wheelin'

Keep on Truckin'

Muck Truck

Mud Buds

Gettin' Down & Dirty

What's a Little Mud Between 2 Friends?

Stuck in the Muck

Muddin'

A Little Dirt Never Hurt Anybody

Rock Hoppin'

Riding High

Lock 'em in!

Macho Machine

gambling

(see also games and money)

Life's a Gamble

Poker Face

Slot Machine Queen

Gotta Know When to Hold 'Em

Ante Up!

I'll Betcha

Let's Make a Deal

The Luck of the Draw

All Bets Are Off

Place Your Bets

My King of Hearts

The Queen of My Heart

---

games

The Games People Play

Fun & Games

Got Game?

Rule #1: Make It Up As You Go

Cheater

Loser!

Sore Losers

It's Not Whether You Win or Lose...

The Championship

Pick a Card... Any Card...

Playing with a Full Deck

A Winning Combination

Power Play

---

gardening

(see also flower)

Harvest Love

How Does Your Garden Grow

Sow Seeds of Kindness

Our Little Sprout

The Pick of the Crop

Pickin' and Grinnin'

Gettin' Down and Dirty

Welcome to My Garden

Home Grown

Garden Angel

Garden Variety

Growing Up

---

gifts

Just What I've Always Wanted

The Perfect Gift

The Past and the Presents

Presents, Presents Everywhere

THANK YOU

Just For You

You REALLY Shouldn't Have

A Gift From the Heart

Big Things Come in Small Packages

Children are God's Greatest Gift

It is Better to Give than to Receive

Under Wraps

The Greatest Gift

All Wrapped Up

---

girl/girls
(see also Daughter)

Girls Just Want to Have Fun

Sugar and Spice and Everything Nice…

Thank Heaven for Perfect Girls

Girls of Grace

Girly Girl

A Classic Beauty

Girls Will Be Girls

SASSY

It's a Girl Thing

Girls Rule, Boys Drool!

DIVA

The Divine Divas

Girl Talk

> **TIP**
> Don't always put the title at the top of the page.

Girl Power

Princess

Our Little Princess

Golden Girls (Blondes)

Drama Queen

Glamour Girls

Girl's Night Out

Pretty in Pink

Little Lady

Queen in Training

Girls' Club

Little Dolls

You Go Girl!

Daddy's Girl

Pure Girl

---

girlfriend

(see also Date and Love)

My One and Only

CRUSH

Puppy Love

A True Romantic

Beauty and the Beast

TOP TITLES and TIPS TOO!

Opposites Attract

Boy Meets Girl

So Far, So Good

You Go, Girlfriend

---

girl scouts

Scouts Honor

Be Prepared

Make New Friends

Scout It Out

---

glasses

(see also Eyes)

SPECtacular

Stay Focused

Set Your Sights High

Looking Glass

A New View

Sights Unseen

A New Outlook on Life

GOLF

FORE!

A Hole in Four

TEErific

The Swinger

Go for the Green

Par for the Course

Eat, Sleep, Golf

Foresight

---

graduation

I Did It!

Congrats Grad!

College Bound

CONGRATULATIONS

Good-bye, East Ridge High

FINALLY

Now I Can Get a Real Job

The Future Looks Bright

Thanks Mom and Dad!

Free at Last!

I'm Outta Here!

Hats Off!

Edgicated

TOP TITLES and TIPS TOO!

Now What?

The Graduate

The Scholar

Follow Your Dreams

If You Can Dream It, You Can Be It

Bye, Bye, Senior High (document the things that will or will not be missed or what is anticipated for the future.)

Reach For the Stars

Believe in Yourself

Beginning a New Journey

I Thought This Day Would Never Come

Opportunity Knocks

All Grown Up

The End.

---

grandchildren

(see also Baby and Child/Children)

They Don't Call 'Em Grand For Nothing

Grandchildren Make Life Grand

Grandchildren Put the Magic Back in Life

My Grandchildren are the Grandest of Them All

Something Grand

TOP TITLES and TIPS TOO!

The Grandest of Them All

Spoiled Rotten by Guess Who?

---

grandfather

(see also grandparents)

My Hero

Call Grandpa: 1-800-I-Want-It

My Granddaddy is the Grandest of Them All

A Day with Poppa is a Priceless Day

Priceless Wisdom

Father of My Father

A PaPaw's Love

Poppa Rules!

A Living Legacy

A Grand Man

There's No Place Like Grandpa's

The "Lap" of Luxury

---

grandmother

(see also grandparents)

Over the River and Through the Woods...

To Grandmommie's House We Go

TOP TITLES and TIPS TOO!

Matriarch

The "Lap" of Luxury

A Timeless Beauty

Call Grandma: 1-800-I-Want-It

Golden Girl

A Woman of Wisdom

Priceless Wisdom

My Grandmother is the Grandest of Them All

A Day in Grandma's Kitchen is a Priceless Day

Snacks Taste Better at Grandma's House

Mother of My Mother

A Grand Woman

A Living Legacy

MeMaw Rules!

A Grandma's Love

There's No Place Like Grandma's

TIP

What do you think about when you envision time spent with your grandparents? Use this special thought as a title for your page. Example: Sunday Evenings and Homemade Ice Cream.

grandparents
(see also grandfather and grandmother)

With Age Comes Wisdom

Grandparents are Angels in Disguise

They Don't Call 'Em Grand For Nothing

Grandparents Make Life Grand

The "Lap" of Luxury

Gray + Hair = Wisdom

Been There, Done That

The Grandest of Them All

Something Grand

---

grow/growing

Growing by Leaps and Bounds

And Then I Blinked My Eyes...

I'm a Big Kid Now

I Remember When...

Growing Like a Weed

TIP
This is a good time to use those extra flower or gardening embellishments.

Get Growing

Done Grown

Ready, Set, Grow!

It's a Small, Small World

"Ruling" the World

Off the Charts

Measuring Up to All Expectations

Monumental Milestones

Our Little Sprout

s-t-r-e-t-c-h

Short & Small, Big & Tall

Just Yesterday…

Sizing Up

The Way Things Were (record characteristics that you'll miss and will always remember)

There's No Turning Back (record the characteristic growth you have seen)

Measuring Up

When I Grow Up

Home Grown

Oh, How They Grow

So Big

Growing, Growing, Grown

Not a Baby Anymore

Growing Pains

All Grown Up

gymnastics

TUMBLIN'

SHOWOFF

It's All in the Execution

It's All in the Landing

Have Balance in Your Life

I'll Bend Over Backwards for You

Flipped Out

Bending the Rules

Bumbling, Tumbling

A Perfect 10

A Balancing Act

Habit

Old Habits are Hard to Break

Again & Again & Again

A Hard Habit to Break

Habitual Offender

Here I Go Again

Irresistible

Hair

Hair Today, Gone Tomorrow

Buzzzz Cut (use bee paper, stickers, or die cuts)

Curl Crazy

Bald is Beautiful

Bad Hair Day

Hairlarious

Wish You Were Hair

A World of Curl

Curly Q

Before & After

A Cut Above the Rest

Just a Trim, Please

My 1st Haircut

The Mane Event

Knot Head

Big Hairy Deal

Rapunzel, Rapunzel

GOLDILOCKS

CURLYLOCKS

Snip, Snip, Snip

Simply to DYE for

On the Cutting Edge

Bed Head

Peach Fuzz

Knotty But Nice

Halloween

So Much Candy, So Little Time

CANDYLAND

BOO!

TRICK or TREAT

WICKED

BOOtiful!

Fright Night

TIP
Using large letters, spell out Halloween across your page. Use a Jack-O-Lantern in place of the "O". The Jack-O-Lantern will be in the center of your page.

TOP TITLES and TIPS TOO!

Witch You Were Here

A Bewitching Evening

Creatures of the Night

Monster Mash

Ghouls Night Out

Boo-Who?

The Cute Spook

Casting a Spell

Scaredy Cat

HAND

HANDle With Care

Look Mom, No Hands!

Loving Hands

I'm a Real Handful

A Hands Down Favorite

A Touch Above the Rest

Hand in Hand

TIP
Stamp your child's hand print on each side of the title to give the appearance that he/she is holding the title.

Right Hand Man

Left Out

Right On!

Thumbs Up!

You're in Good Hands (tell what lengths have been taken to take care of your subject)

Hold on with All Your Heart

A Good Rule of Thumb

The Cutest Baby Around...Hands Down!

So HANDsome

Gimme a Hand, Please

Hold On

Caught Red-Handed

Handmade

(see Art, Baking, Crafts and Sewing)

Hanukkah

Shining Bright

Oh, Dreidel, Dreidel, Dreidel

The Magical Menorah

Eight Lights, Eight Nights

TOP TITLES and TIPS TOO!

The Power of Light

Feast of Dedication

Festival of Lights

Happiness

(see also Laughter)

On Top of the World

Don't Worry, Be Happy

Floating on Cloud Nine

Happiness is…

The Joy of Having It All

Immeasurable Pleasure

Joy to the World

Beauty Gives Joy

Color Me Happy

Rejoice

Cheerful

Pure Bliss

Happy as a Clam

Happy Days

Good Times

TOP TITLES and TIPS TOO!

Harvest
(see Fall, Gardening and Pumpkins)

Hat

Hats Off to You

The Mad Hatter

You've Flipped Your Lid!

Oh, That Hat! That Hat!

Hat Tricks

Heart

(see also Love)

Heart to Heart

A Work of Heart

My Heart and Soul

The Heart of the Country

Be Still, My Heart

A Gift from the Heart

TIP
Check this out! After using a template for the outline, draw a grid over the letters, then fill in every other box with contrasting colors.

• 103 •

TOP TITLES and TIPS TOO!

Follow Your Heart

Home is Where the Heart Is

I Love You With All My Heart

The Key to My Heart

The Heart of the Home

An Affair of the Heart

Queen of Hearts

Let Your Heart Dance

...with All My Heart

SweetHeart

Heartwarming

Heaven

A Gift from Above

Heaven Sent

Our Bundle from Heaven

The Promised Land

A Blessing

A Match Made in Heaven

Heaven on Earth

Heritage

(see also Family and Memories)

A Grandma is an Antique Little Girl

A Classic

Yesteryear

An Oldie but Goodie

Beauty From the Past

From Past to Present

From Days Gone By

Making History

Then and Now

A Step Back in Time (use the stickers of old-fashioned shoes that come on most heritage sticker sheets)

A Timeless Treasure

Generation to Generation

The Rest is History

Life in the Past Lane

Golden Days

Through the Years

A Legacy

Vintage

Priceless Heirlooms

It All Starts and Ends With Family

TOP TITLES and TIPS TOO!

Travel Back in Time (this is a good chance to use the old-fashioned suitcase stickers that are often included on heritage sticker sheets)

Nostalgia

The Past + The Present = The Future

Hiking

Happy Trails

Take A Hike

A Walk On the Wild Side

Welcome to Our Neck of the Woods

Trail of Good Times

Trail and Error

Headed Down the Wrong Path

Hot on the Trail

Head for the Hills

Hot on the Trail

Out & About

The Path Taken

My Chosen Path

TIP
When using a single word as your title, use title blocks, alternating themed stickers and the letters within the word.

TOP TITLES and TIPS TOO!

Trail Blazers

Nature Hike

Hike It Up

Hittin' the Trail

Hockey

(see also sports)

He Shoots! He Scores!

Crunching Ice

Iceman

Hot on the Ice

I Have a Goal in Life

GOAL!

SCORE!

Cold as Ice

Playing It Cool

Too Cool

Home/House

(see also Remodeling)

There's No Place Like Home

Home Is Where The Heart Is

TOP TITLES and TIPS TOO!

Love Makes a House a Home

Homemade Memories

The Heart of the Home

The Comforts of Home

Home Again

Small House, Big Charm

The Great Indoors

If These Walls Could Talk…

Dream Home

The Home Stretch

Honey, I'm Home!

Fixer Upper

Our Dream House

We've Moved

New Address, New Attitude

Cozy and Charming

The American Dream

House + Love = Home

Our Mansion

Our Lil' Cottage

TIP
Scatter the words of your title over the page, being careful to keep the phrase legible. This will draw your eyes across the layout.

TOP TITLES and TIPS TOO!

Room to Breathe

Great Things Come in Small Packages

Home Sweet Home

Home Sweet Apartment

Home School

(see also SCHOOL)

Home Is Where The School Is

Home Sweet Home School

Horse

(see also COWBOY)

Buckaroo

Horse Power

Beauty in Motion

Nature's Galloping Beauty

Whoa!

Hot to Trot

Horse Play

Horsin' Around

Straight from the Horse's Mouth

Giddyup

Round 'Em Up

TOP TITLES and TIPS TOO!

Why the Long Face?

The Mane Event

Hug

Bear Hug

Cuddle Buddies

Cute-N-Cuddly

Cheek to Cheek

XOXOXO

As Cuddly as a Teddy Bear

Cuddles and Kisses

Heart to Heart

Hugs & Kisses

Lean On Me

Friends Stick Together

Heaven on Earth

Heart Warming

My Main Squeeze

Close Encounter of the Best Kind

An Expression of Love

All Wrapped Up

Too Close for Comfort

The Greatest Gift

A Random Act of Kindness

Hold Me Close

Let Me Go!

Love One Another

Embrace Life

A Special Hug for You, From Me

Hunting

Daddy's Little Dear

Huntin' Buddies

Big Shot

On the Hunt

The Buck Stops Here

Hunting Season

BULLSEYE!

Sharpshooter

Buck Fever

My Deer

What a Shot!

The Thrill of the Hunt

ice cream

Ice Cream Weather

It Takes a Lickin'

SWEET

Sweets for the Sweeties

Licking the Heat

Hey, Good Lickin'

A Taste of Summer

What a Cool Idea!

My Sundae Best

The Ice Cream Social

illness

(see also doctor)

Sick Chick

Laughter is the Best Medicine

Caught a Bug

Road to Recovery

Catch the Fever

Share & Share Alike

TOP TITLES and TIPS TOO!

Treat with TLC

On the Mend

Take Care

Lovesick

Homesick

Life is Fragile. Handle With Prayer.

In Sickness and In Health...

Prescription: Tender Loving Care

Feeling Under the Weather

Love Conquers All

A Picture of Health

Moanin' and Groanin'

Oh, My Aching....

independence Day/Patriotism

All American

All American Kid

American Made

Let Freedom Ring

TIP
Substitute a name or place in any recognizable phrase.
Example: Fast Times at East Ridge High.

TOP TITLES and TIPS TOO!

An All American Good Time

Star-Spangled Fun

United We Stand

Our Lil' Firecracker

A Sparkling Personality

FREEDOM

Old Glory

Americana

Proud to be an American

A Festive Fourth

God Bless America

Happy Birthday, America

The Land That I Love

---

injury
(see also Doctor)

OUCH!

OOPS!

Life is Fragile. Handle With Care.

Trial and Error

My Boo-Boo

Mommy Cried More Than Me

The Road To Recovery

Brace Yourself

My Big Break

Treat with TLC

On the Mend

On the Cutting Edge

Cuttin' Up

A Cut Above the Rest

You Keep Me in Stitches

Sore Loser

Take Care

All Stitched Up

You Keep Me In Stitches

Prescription: Tender Loving Care

The CASTing Couch

First Aid

The Agony of DeFEET

Moanin' and Groanin'

Oh, My Aching...

Time Heals All Wounds

Gimme a Break

EMERGENCY

TOP TITLES and TIPS TOO!

Inspirational

Live in the Moment

Reach for the Stars

I Think I Can, I Think I Can, I Can!

Stop and Smell the Roses

Notice the Little Things

Cherish the Moment

Believe in Miracles

Do You Believe?

Make a Wish

Heaven on Earth

Count Your Blessings

My Inspiration

JOB

(see Money and Work)

Jumping

A Leap of Faith

By Leaps and Bounds

Growing by Leaps and Bounds

Popping Up All Over the Place

Jumping Out of the Frying Pan, Into the Fire

Feeling Froggy? Jump!

Jump for Joy

A Hop, Skip, and Jump Away

Bouncing Baby Boy

Don't Worry, Be Hoppy

Is This Leap Year?

What Goes Up, Must Come Down

Uplifting

kindergarten

(see also SCHOOL)

Mommy Cried, I Played

Making New Friends

It's Just the Beginning

KISS

Butterfly Kisses

A Kiss for Luck

S.W.A.K.

HOTLIPS

The Kiss of Death

Turn the Other Cheek

Ooh! Cooties!

Kiss Me Baby

Cute Couple

Tanner and Talisa, sitting in a tree, K-I-S-S-I-N-G

Planting Twolips

Kissing Cousins

Give Me Some Sugar, Baby

Heaven on Earth

The Greatest Gift

Kiss & Tell (be sure to tell the story behind the kiss!)

Hello, Sweetlips!

Pucker Up

As Sweet as Sugar

A Kiss is Just a Kiss

A Random Act of Kindness

An Expression of Love

XOXOXO

Hugs and Kisses

SMOOCHING

Simply Irresistible

Love One Another

Cuddles and Kisses

KITE

Flying High

Up, Up, and Away

High in the Sky

Aim High

Go Fly a Kite

If at First You Don't Succeed, Try, Try Again

KNOT

Knotty But Nice

All Tied Up at the Moment

The Ties That Bind

I Think Knot

Knot Me

Knot Head

TOP TITLES and TIPS TOO!

Laugh/Laughing/Laughter
(see also Happiness)

Giggle Giggle Giggle

Live. Love. Laugh.

Tickled Pink

Laughter is the Best Medicine

Your Laughter is Contagious

You Keep Me in Stitches

We Laughed… We Cried…

What a Sense of Humor!

It's Just an Expression

Love
(see also Heart)

Love is in the Air

Love in Bloom

Young Love

Puppy Love

My Best Friend, My True Love

A Budding Romance

I Wish You Love

Love at First Sight

Unconditionally

Let Love Bloom

Live. Love. Laugh.

You're Perfect (for me!)

The Love Bug

Love Hurts

A Life of Love

Always and Forever

An Expression of Love

A Love Connection

Just the Two of Us

The Power of Love

The Greatest Gift

Two Hearts, One Love

My Love

Ain't Love Grand?

Lovebirds

Lovesick

TIP
Title this page with a line from "your song."

The Love of My Life

Love Letters

A Match Made in Heaven

World's Happiest Couple

I'll Love You Forever

Unconditional Love

Forever and Ever

Everlasting Love

My Knight in Shining Armor

I Love You With All My Heart

Love Makes Life Complete

My One and Only

True Love

Love Conquers All

He Loves Me, He Loves Me Not

How Do I Love Thee? Let Me Count the Ways...

Magic

Spellbound

This Magic Moment

Intrigue & Mystery

Abracadabra

And for My Next Trick...

Hocus Pocus

Magical Mystery

Make-Believe

(see Cowboy, Fairytale and Pirate)

Martial Arts

Freestyle

The Graceful Warrior

The Power Within

My Side Kick

Self-Defense

Invincible

The Fist of Fury

It's Not Just for Kicks

Memories

Memory Lane

Memories in the Making

Memory is the Power to Gather Roses in the Winter

Memories for a Lifetime

Keeping the Memory Alive

I Will Remember You

The Glory Days

Live, Love, Laugh…Remember

Thanks for the Memories

Homemade Memories

Days are Fleeting, the Memories are Forever

Magical Memories

Remember When…

These are the Times to Remember

The Way It Was

Cherished Days

Reflections

A Legacy

More Memorable Moments

Priceless…

For Old Times Sake

Gone But Not Forgotten

The Good Ol' Days

I Remember When…

Where Did the Time Go?

Through the Years

Seems Like Yesterday

Treasured Thoughts

Everyday Moments Become Cherished Memories

Men

It Must Be a Guy Thing

Manly Man

A Jack of All Trades

A Good Man is Hard to Find

My Knight in Shining Armor

Men Will Be Men

Men Will Be Boys

Tough Guy

The King

Macho Man

A Super Man

Military

Ready, Willing, and Able (U.S. ARMY)

Wings of Victory (U.S. Air Force)

TOP TITLES and TIPS TOO!

Above and Beyond (U.S. Air Force)

Proud to Serve (U.S. Navy)

Our Hero

Military Man

Stand at Ease

The Unsung Hero

Rank and File

Above and Beyond the Call of Duty

...and Our Flag was Still There.

All American

Let Freedom Ring

Freedom Fighters

United We Stand

Tie a Yellow Ribbon

A Fight for Freedom

War. What Is It Good For? (Voice your opinion on war; For historical purposes, state the opposing opinion as well.)

Shore-ly Missed

Duty Calls

Salute!

Thank You.

MILK

MOOre Milk, Please

Milk Mustache

Milkin' it for All it's Worth

Milk Does a Body Good

Got Milk?

Udderly Delicious

Udderly Adorable

Money

Show Me the Money

$$$$$

Cha-Ching!

MOOLAH

Ooh la la! Moolah!

Right on the Money

Rolling in the Dough

I'm Rich!

Who Wants To Be A Millionaire?

Rich in the Things that Matter

Pricele$$

A Penny for Your Thoughts

Money Machine

I Owe It All to You

Big Spender

Deep in Debt

Cash Flow

Penny Pincher

I Owe! I Owe! Off to Work I Go!

For Richer, For Poorer

The Buck Stops Here

The Lap of Luxury

Monkey

Going Bananas

Monkey on My Back

Hear No Evil, See No Evil

Monkey Business

Monkey-ing Around

Monkey See, Monkey Do

TOP TITLES and TIPS TOO!

MOON
(see also SLEEP)

The Man in the Moon

Goodnight

MOTHER

Like Mother, Like Daughter

Mommy and Me

Every Mother is a Working Woman

Unconditional Love

Always Caring, Always Giving, Always Loved

A Mother's Touch

Mother's Loving Ways

A Mom of All Trades

A Mother's Work is Never Done

A Mother is a Girl's Best Friend

The Best Friend a Daughter Could Ever Have

The Queen and Her Princess

A Special Lady

"Stay" at Home Mom? Ha!

The Queen of All Mums

Mommy's Day

TOP TITLES and TIPS TOO!

The "Lap" of Luxury

My Guidance

A Living Legacy

I Owe it All to You

Head Honcho

A Mother's Love

Being a Mother Means...

Lifelong Friend & Mother

Mother Knows Best

MOTHER-in-LAW

My Other Mother

Mother by Marriage

His Mother, My Friend

MOTOrcycLe

Born to be Wild

A Boy & His Bike

Hog Wild

Hog Heaven

The Rambler

I'm Two Tired

---

movies/television

That's the Ticket

A Real Character

Lights! Camera! Action!

Coming to a Television Near You

Now Showing

The Reel Deal

FANtastic (list your favorite stars/shows/movies)

Everybody's a Critic (make a list of favorite shows and what you like about them, or document your child's reaction when you turn on YOUR favorite show)

Drama Queen

Theater of Dreams

As Seen on TV

TIP
Use your television schedule for ideas. For example, if your layout has a sports theme, check out the titles of the shows on the Sports channel. Also try watching the Home channel for house projects.

TOP TITLES and TIPS TOO!

TV Land

Couch Potatoes

Baby Couch Potato

Watch This!

What to Watch

Tube Time

MULTIPLES

(see also sibling)

Double Trouble

Two's Company

Two of a Kind

Seeing Double

Like 2 Peas in a Pod

Double Exposure

Triple Trouble

Three's Company

Three's a Crowd

Three of a Kind

Copy Cats

Split Personalities

Womb-mates

Who's Who?

And Baby Makes 3 & 4 & 5

Three's a Charm

Thrice is Nice

Twice as Nice

Triple Time

The More the Merrier

The Gang's All Here

3X the Work = 3X the Love

Three Dimensional

Thank Heaven for Little Babies

A Thriving Threesome

Baby Bonanza

Miraculous Multiples

Two at a Time

Oh, Baby! Baby! Baby!

Two for One

Two by Two

Doubles (use those extra tennis stickers)

Just the Two of Us

Love Times Two

It's a Boy! & A Girl! & A Girl!

Double Duty

Sugar and Spice (list their differences)

Dynamic Duo

Adorable Duo

TOP TITLES and TIPS TOO!

Twice the Fun

Double Up

MUSIC

I've Got Rhythm

Feel the Rhythm

Encore! Encore!

Let the Music Play

Rock-N-Roll

Songbird

Let Your Heart Sing

RadioActive

Band of Brothers

The Entertainer

The Sound of Music

Consistent C

A Little Bit Country, A Little Bit Rock-N-Roll

TIP
Overlapping a special photo with the words (or at least one letter) of the title will create an automatic focus point.

A Band of Gold

Sing Along

Music to My Ears

Practice Makes Perfect

Practice Makes Better

Practice, Practice, Practice

Name

What's in a Name?

The Name Game

Who's Who?

You Can Just Call Me...

Namesake

A Rose by Any Other Name...

A Special Name for a Special Boy

An Unique Name for a Unique Girl

Introducing...

Giving A New Meaning to an Old Name

Hello! My Name Is:

TOP TITLES and TIPS TOO!

Who Am I?

Cute is My Middle Name

Guess Who?

Nature

It's Only Natural

The Great Outdoors

Nature Boy

On the Lookout

Nature's Sanctuary

Naturally...

Neighbor

A Good Neighbor is Hard to Find

Love Thy Neighbor as Thyself -Rom. 13:9

To Know Them is to Love Them

> **TIP**
> Title with your street name or the apartment complex name & number.

TOP TITLES and TIPS TOO!

The Girl Next Door

Neighbor vs. Neighbor

Newspaper

Extra! Extra!

News Flash

Front Page News

Making News

Have You Heard the Good News?

New Year

(see also Party)

Out With the Old, In With the New

The Future Looks Bright

CELEBRATION

Celebrate Good Times

WELCOME 2005

GOODBYE 2004

I Resolve to...

Good Times are Here to Stay

A Big End to a Big Year

TOP TITLES and TIPS TOO!

Auld Lang Syne

The Year in Review

10,9,8,7,6,5,4,3,2,1.....

A Great Start for a Great Year to Come

NOAH'S ARK

Two by Two

Flooded With Blessings

All Aboard!

NUDE

Naked Again

Is it Cold in Here or Is it Just Me?

The Nude Kid on the Block

Bare Your Soul

Show & Tell

At the Crack of Dawn

The Bottom Line

Are Ya' Naked?

As Free as a Bird

SASSY

Bare Bottom

Centerfold Material

BAREly 2 years old

BAREly covered

odor

SCENTsational

Lil' Stinker

Shoo!

park

(see also picnic, slide and swing)

A Day at the Park

A Walk in the Park

The Great Outdoors

Park Pals

Grasshoppers

Party

Let's Party

It's Party Time

The More the Merrier

How Did It Get So Late, So Early?

You're Invited

It's My Party and I'll Cry If I Want To

The Life of the Party

In High Spirits

Party Girl

Party Animal

Raise the Roof

Eat, Drink, and be Merry

Party Central

Celebrate!

Passover

Shining Bright

Feast of the Unleavened Bread

Matzoh Meal

Freedom Festival

The Season of Freedom

Peach

Peach Fuzz

Peachy Keen

Life's Just Peachy

What a Peach

Pet
(see also specific animals)

Our Zoo

Petting Zoo

It's a Boy! and a Girl and a Girl and a Boy!

Pampered Pet

Bless the Beasts and the Children

TOP TITLES and TIPS TOO!

My Pet, My Friend, My Baby

I'm Fur-fect

My Furry Companion

Unconditional Love

Pet Peeve (tell of your pet's quirky characteristics)

PHOTOGRAPHS/PHOTOGRAPHY

Picture This

SMILE

Say "Cheese"

Strike A Pose

Everyday Moments

Get the Picture?

Freeze Frame

Camera Shy

En Vogue

FotoFun

TIP
Using a special interest magazine about your subject, scan the table of content pages. Article headlines make great page titles.

Framed!

What a Shot!

Picture Perfect

Priceless...

O.K., Take It

Hammin' It Up

Capture the Moment

Capture the Memories

Pretty as a Picture

Miles of Smiles

Freeze Frame

Superstar

I'm a Star!

A Picture is Worth a Thousand Words

Let's See What Develops

Shutterbug

Big Shot

Lights, Camera, Action!

Grin and Bear It

Ain't I Cute?

Show Us Those Pearly Whites

TOP TITLES and TIPS TOO!

piano
(see also music)

Baby Grand

Baby, I'm Grand

Baby, Ain't Life Grand

Practice Makes Perfect

RECITAL

---

picnic

Picnic in the Park

A Taste of Summer

NicPicking

Life is a Picnic

Life's No Picnic

No Ifs, Ants, or Bugs About It

Family Picnic

TIP
Don't forget the easy option of using title blocks (small squares of colored cardstock) under your letters for a neat look.

Pie
(see also Baking)

Cutie Pie

Sweetie Pie

SWEET TOOTH

Pig

This Little Piggy...

OINK OINK OINK

Porky

When Pigs Fly...

Pig Sty

Hog Heaven

Hog Wild

Pirate

Hidden Treasures

A Treasure of Memories

Out to Sea

Our Little Treasure

Walk the Plank

TOP TITLES and TIPS TOO!

Aye, Aye, Captain

Captain Colt

Play/Program
(see also star)

Hollywood, Here I Come

All the World's a Stage

The World is My Stage

A Real Character

Drama Queen

Theater of Dreams

Drama

Center Stage

Break a Leg

There's No Business Like Show Business

Child's Play

Lights, Camera, Action!

POOL
(see swimming)

TOP TITLES and TIPS TOO!

Pregnancy

Ready, Set, Wait

Expecting the Best

The Home Stretch

It's a Boy! Or a Girl!

Pregnancy Weight

Weighting for Baby

Any Day Now!

Anxiously Awaiting

What NOT to Say to a Pregnant Woman (We all have these stories, and even though they are not very funny at the time, we may laugh at the nerve of the people later.)

Weighting Anxiously

With Child

Advice I Received... (Don't forget to record who said it.)

Prom

Memories in the Making

A Night to Remember

Dancing the Night Away

The Belle of the Ball

Let Your Heart Dance

TOP TITLES and TIPS TOO!

Best Dressed

Oh, What a Night

Dream Date

Cute Couple

How Did It Get So Late, So Early?

Pumpkin

Lil' Pumpkin

Pumpkin Patch

Pickin' Pumpkins

Picking and Grinning

Carvin' Time

A Sign of the Season

The Pick of the Crop

Can I Pick 'Em or What?

Punkin Pickin

Pumpkin Bumpkin

TIP

When creating a prom layout, use the prom's theme song for the title.

PUZZLE

The Missing Link

Hmm, Puzzle-ing

It's a Puzzle to Me, Too

Falling to Pieces

The Last Piece of the Puzzle

RABBIT

There's No Bunny Like You

Somebunny Special

Hopping Down the Bunny Trail

Hippity!Hoppity!Happy!

Somebunny Loves Me

Race/Racing

(see also Driving)

Speed Racer

Pit Stop

Gentlemen, Start Your Engines

TOP TITLES and TIPS TOO!

Race Day

From Start to Finish

The Grand Prix

Fast Friends

Like the Speed of Light

LIGHTNING

The Need for Speed

The Race Is On

Built for Speed

Life in the Fast Lane

It's Off to the Races!

Rafting

WHITEWATER

Riding the Rapids

Man Overboard

Row, Row, Row Your Raft

A Whitewater Misadventure

Rain

TOP TITLES and TIPS TOO!

Our Rainy Day Sunshine

Singing in the Rain

A Damp Dark Day

Look on the Bright Side

Showered With Love

Sprinkles On Top

Sprinkled With Love

Rainy Day Fun

Raindrops Keep Fallin' On My Head

Sprinkle Sprinkle Sprinkle

Feeling Under the Weather

Rain, Rain, Go Away, Come Again Another Day

April Showers Bring May Flowers

Rain, Rain, Go Away

It's Raining, It's Pouring

DOWNPOUR

Raining Cats and Dogs

When It Rains, It Pours

Showers Bring Flowers

Get Your Feet Wet

Let it Rain

Puddle Play

A Splashing Good Time

TOP TITLES and TIPS TOO!

Spring Showers

A Flood of Blessings

A Flood of Misery

Rainbow

Look on the Bright Side...

Rainy Day Reward

Follow Your Rainbow

Color My World

Color Me Silly

A Colorful Personality

Somewhere Over the Rainbow

Better than a Pot of Gold

Our Little Leprechaun

The Many Colors of Rachel

Show Your True Colors

Chasing Rainbows

Retirement

FINALLY!

Now What?

I Thought This Day Would Never Come

What Will They Ever Do Without Me?

I'm Outta Here!

I've Earned It!

Bye-Bye Tension, Hello Pension

Quittin' Time

I'm Tired Again

Do What You Like, Like What You Do

Time for a Little R&R

Professional Tourist

Well Deserved

Reunion

How Long Has It Been?

It's Been Too Long

Reunited After All These Years

Where Have You Been All My Life?

Together At Last

I've Missed You

Remember Me?

'Til We Meet Again

TOP TITLES and TIPS TOO!

ROCK/ROCKing CHAiR

A Milestone

Rock-N-Roll

Rock Bottom

Boulder and Beautiful

Rock-A-Bye Baby

Between a Rock and a Hard Place

Rocking-N-Roll

We're Rocking Now!

A Rocking Good Time

ROLLing over
(see also FiRSTS)

Over and Over Again

Flipped Out

Rolling Through Life

Roll-y Poll-y

Rock-n-ROLL

Just Roll with it, Baby

I'm on a Roll Now!

Run/Running

(see also Race)

Ready, Set, GO!

Going, Going, Gone

Goin' Places

Runnin' Wild

Road Runner

From Start to Finish

It Runs in the Family

Get a Move On, Baby

Built for Speed

Fast Friends

Up and Runnin'

On the Move

On the Run

I'll Be There in a Jiffy!

Run Away

HUSTLE

I'm Outta Here!

Where's the Fire?

Slow Down!

Beauty in Motion

Run Like the Wind

Sad

(see also crying)

Why the Long Face?

Soooo Sad

Sorrowful Day

Don't Worry, Be Happy

Color Me Sad

Santa Claus

I Believe

Claus-trophobia

Dear Santa, (write a letter explaining why you should be on his nice list or apologizing for why you are on his naughty list.)

Santa and Me

TIP
Include a list of what your child asked for this year and what was received.

TOP TITLES and TIPS TOO!

Naughty or Nice?

A Jolly Old Soul

Jolly Little Souls

Cheeks Like Cherries

Do You Believe?

HO HO HO

Dear Santa, I've Been Good

Santa's Helper

Nevermind!

HO HO NO!

Our Little Elves

A Holly, Jolly Christmas

Our 1st Meeting

The Bearded Stranger

Jolly Holidays

---

scare

BOO!

Did You Hear That?

What Was That?

Scaredy Cat

TOP TITLES and TIPS TOO!

Hold Me

Eeeeeeek!

SCHOOL

School Spirit

School Days

School Daze

Back 2 School

My Favorite Subject

When is Recess?

Hittin' the Books

I've Got a Lot of Class

Class-y

Do Your Homework

Getting Edgicated

Bus STOP!

Best of the Class

The World's Cutest Student

Study Buddies

The Wheels on the Bus

It All Adds Up

Making the Grade

Reading, Writing, Arithmetic

School is Cool!

Too Cool for School

Hooray for the First Day!

When is Lunch?

ABC's and 123's

S is for School

Making Progress

Future Honor Student

Honor Student in Training

Genius in Training

A Star Student

Head of the Class

All Grown Up

TIP

Title this layout with the school's name, initials, mascot, or motto. Don't take for granted that future generations will know what school your subject went to.

Another suggestion: Substitute the more common "A is for Apple" with any letter and word that is appropriate for your layout, Example: D is for Dylan or L is for Lovin' School.

scrapbooking

(see also Memories and Stickers)

Good 'til the Last Crop

Crop Everything

A Scrappin' Good Time

Saving Memories, Making New Ones

Saving Memories, Making Friends

Crop 'til You Drop

SCRAPAHOLICS

Just Call Me "Scrappy"

Made With Love

Capture the Memories

On the Cutting Edge

Ready! Set! CROP!

All About Me

From the Pages of My Mind

How Adorn-able

A Passion for Scrappin'

The Past, The Present, for the Future

And the Story Begins…

Preserving the Past

Discovering, Preserving, Celebrating Family

TOP TITLES and TIPS TOO!

Cuttin' Up

For Generations to Come...

sewing

(see also crafts)

Sew Much Fabric, Sew Little Time

Cute as a Button

Sew Adorable

Sew Much Fun

Cut From the Same Cloth

A Stitch in Time...

You Keep Me in Stitches

I See a Pattern Here

Sew What!

shine

Dazzling

All that Glitters is Not Gold

Look on the Bright Side

TOP TITLES and TIPS TOO!

SHOE

(see also FEET)

My Heart and Sole

Knotty but Nice

Kick Up Your Heels

Put Yourself in My Shoes

Put Your Best Foot Forward

I Think Knot

All Tied Up at the Moment

The Ties that Bind

One, Two, Tie Your Shoes…

Knot Me!

Knot Head

Shoo!

SHOPPING

Born to Shop

Shopping is in Our Genes

We Came, We Shopped, We Conquered

Shop-a-holic

Let's Make a Deal

Shop 'til You Drop

Shopping Spree

Spending Spree

When Ya' Gotta Have It, Ya' Just Gotta Have It

SPLURGE

Bargain Hunters

Retail Therapy

On the Hunt

The Sale of the Century

Budget Bustin'

Shop 'Til You Drop

Eat, Sleep, Shop

shower

Showered with Love

April Showers Bring May Babies

The Shower of the Century

A Very Gifted Baby

A Spring Shower

Expecting Showers

Tip

For special events, pull your title from an invitation or the theme of the occasion.

TOP TITLES and TIPS TOO!

Prepared for the Big Day

You are Invited

Ooh! Aah!

Gifted

Sibling

(see also Brother, Family, Multiples and Sister)

Sibling Rivalry

Sibling Revelry

Inseparable

Inseparable Siblings

In the Middle of It All

Sibling Similarities

Sensational Siblings

Built-in Friends

Partners in Crime

I'm the Big Sister

The More the Merrier

Count Your Blessings

sick

(see illness)

silly

Why Be Normal? (Zig-zag the word "Normal",
or write it upside down)

Whimsical

Funny Face

Fun-Duh-Mental

Kiddin' Around

The Fourth Stooge

Sooooooo Silly

sister

(see also girl, family and sibling)

My Sister, My Friend

Sisters Since the Beginning, Friends 'Til the End

Sister, Sister

A Sister Understands

A Sister's Love

A Sister is a Lifelong Friend

TOP TITLES and TIPS TOO!

I'm the Big Sister

What are Big Sisters for?

Skate

Skate into Winter

Gliding Through Life

Glidin' Along

Rollin' Along

Crunching Ice

Hot on the Ice

COOL!

Freestyling

Just Roll with it, Baby

Skating on Thin Ice

Roller Derby

Slippin' and Slidin'

Fast Friends

Skateboard

Glidin' Through Life

Gliding Along

Freestyling

Skate Mania

Fast Friends

---

skiing

Hittin' the Slopes

It's All Downhill from Here

Hopping Down the Bunny Slope

Snow Bunny

Winter Wonderland

Water Whimsy

What a Rush!

Crunching Ice

Iceman

Ride the Wave

Just Gliding Through

Skiing Through Life

On a Downhill Slide

Hot on the Ice

COOL!

SLEEP

Sleeping Beauty

American Idle

Rest Assured

Going Undercover

Back to Sleep

Bed Rest

Son Up to Son Down

Sweet Dreams are Made of This

All I Have To Do Is Dream

While You Were Sleeping

Sweet Dreams Sweet Angel

Siesta

Just Relax

Beautiful Dreamer

Rock-a-bye Baby

Snuggle

Sweet Slumber

Sandman

Lullaby

Tranquility

Dream Wizard

Do Not Disturb

The Weary Traveler

Dream Chaser

I am a Dream Come True

The Princess of Dreams

Sleep Tight, Sweet Prince

Lights Out!

You're So Dreamy!

Shhhh

Zzzzz

Recharging

Nite Nite

Shh…Angel Sleeping

This Is How An Angel Sleeps

A Lullabye Moment

Counting Sheep

It's Raining, It's Pouring, the Old Man is Snoring

Now I Lay Me Down To Sleep

Sweet Dreams

Sleepy Head

Early to Bed, Early to Rise

Follow Your Dreams

Sleeping In

Bed Head

All is Calm

As Snug as a Bug in a Rug

TOP TITLES and TIPS TOO!

Life is but a Dream

May All Your Dreams Come True

---

slide

Slip Slidin' Away

Slide Into Summer

Sliding Through Life

On a Downhill Slide

What Goes Up Must Come Down

---

smile

Shine On

Smiley Face

Joy to the World

It's Just an Expression

An "Expression" of Love

Say, "Cheese"

Miles of Smiles

TOP TITLES and TIPS TOO!

snake

Sssssnakes

Here's the Ssssssssstory....

Snakes and Snails and Puppy Dog Tails

---

snow/winter

Our Little Eskimos

Polar Bears

Snow Much Fun

Playing It Cool

Snow Angel

Snow Baby

Snow Day

B-L-I-Z-Z-A-R-D

Let it Snow, Let it Snow, Let it Snow

As Cool as Ice

Old Man Winter

The Shimmer Season

Jack Frost

The Ice Age

Deep Freeze

The Essence of Winter

TOP TITLES and TIPS TOO!

Winter Wonderland

Brrrrr!!!

Too Cool

If We Could Freeze Time...

Cold Days, Warm Hearts

Warmest Wishes

A Child of All Seasons

A Sign of the Season

BUNDLED

Snow Bunnies

No Two are Alike

FROSTY

The Snowball Champion

The 2004 Snowball Fight Championship

---

soccer

SCORE

GOAL

I Get a Kick Out of You

Gettin' Our Kicks

Playing the Field

I Have a Goal in Life

Hands Off!

Just for Kicks

SOCKS

Shoo!

Sock It To Me

You Knock My Socks Off

Kick Up Your Heels

son

(see also Baby, Boy and Child)

The Son that Brightens My Day

Our Little Sonshine

Like Father, Like Son

Lifelong Friend and Son

He's Our Heart and Soul

A Son is Heaven on Earth

Love from Son Up to Son Down

Lifelong Friend & Son

A Son is Love

special

To Know Me is to Love Me

The Eighth Wonder of the World

Like Nothing Else on Earth

I Owe it All to You

What Matters Most

A Picture is Worth a Thousand Words

An Original

Inspiring

One of a Kind

My Life, My Love, My World

Mine, All Mine

Cherish

The Moment

Magical

This Magic Moment

Extraordinary

Enchantment

Pricele$$

Picture Perfect

Perfection

Especially Special

The Wonder Of It All

That's Incredible!

How Wonderful!

A Day to Remember

Right Now Only Happens Once

Live in the Moment

Heaven on Earth

Simply Me

One Moment in Time

Perfect in Every Way

---

spider

Itsy Bitsy Spider

CREEPY CRAWLY

Oh, What a Tangled Web We Weave...

---

sports

(see also specific sports)

ALL STAR

My Little All-star

Go! Fight! Win!

The Sports Page

TOP TITLES and TIPS TOO!

Havin' A Ball

Team Spirit

Team Player

Got Game?

The Games People Play

Fun & Games

Athletic Supporter

Born to Play

Get in the Game

A Team Effort

Ball Babes

Ball Buds

The Essence of Team Spirit

Power Play

Play-by-Play

MVP

We're #1

Practice Makes Perfect

Practice, Practice, Practice

Sore Losers

Be A Winner

It's Not Whether You Win or Lose…

We'll Get 'Em Next Time

V-I-C-T-O-R-Y

The Champs

---

spring

Spring Has Sprung

Spring to Life

Spring Fever

Spring Cleaning Time

Spring Fling

Love in Bloom

Swing Into Spring

Spring Into Summer

Spring Into Action

The Essence of Spring

It's a Spring Thing

April Showers Bring May Flowers

Spring Cleaning

TIP

If you have ever had a doodle-ing style of writing (bubble letters, for example), use it to give the title your personal touch.

STANDING/PULLING UP

(see also FIRSTS)

What Goes Up Must Come Down

Will the Real Cody Please Stand Up?

Standing Room Only

A Real Stand Up Guy

Standing Proud

Stand Tall

Ready for Action

A Balancing Act

Vertical

Reaching New Heights

Steady Does It

What's Up, Baby?

Taking a Stand

Stand for What You Believe In

Stand Strong or You'll Fall for Anything

Pull-ups

I Stand Out in a Crowd

STAR

My Little All-Star

Born to be a Star

Hitch Your Wagon to a Star

Twinkle Twinkle

A Shining Star

SUPERSTAR

I'm a Star!

Star Power

A Star is Born

Make a Wish...

Stargazer

Starstruck

Star-crossed

When You Wish Upon a Star...

Reach for the Stars

A Star Performance

The Star of the Show

sticker

Stick to What You Know

Memories that Stick

I'm Stuck on You

Stick 'em Up

TOP TITLES and TIPS TOO!

A Sticky Situation

S-T-I-C-K-Y

ST. PATRICK'S DAY

Our Little Leprechaun

My Lucky Charm

Lucky Me

Lil' Leprechaun

The Luck of the Irish

Dance a Jig

Better Than a Pot of Gold

PINCHED

STRAWBERRY

A Berry Special Boy

I'm in a Jam

A Strawberry Blonde

TOP TITLES and TIPS TOO!

Stroller

Strollin' Along

I'm Outta Here!

Let's Get Out of Here

CRUISIN'

Takin' a Stroll

Roll With It, Baby

Summer
(see also sun)

Lazy Summer Days

Hot Summer Days

Summer Fun

Barefoot and Fancy Free

HOT HOT HOT

Boys of Summer

Summer Lovin' Girls

Sun-Kissed

Too Cool to be Hot

Some Like it Hot

The Dog Days of Summer

Spring Into Summer

TOP TITLES and TIPS TOO!

Things are Heating Up

The Essence of Summer

---

sun

(see also sunbathing)

You Light Up My Life

You Are My Sunshine

Fun in the Sun

Mr. Sun, Shine On Me

The Light of My Life

Friends in Sunshine and in Shade

Look on the Bright Side

The Bright Spot in My Day

Celestial

Shine On

Sizzling

The Son that Brightens My Day

Sunny Sensations

Walking on Sunshine

SUNBATHING/SUNBURN

Soakin' Up Some Rays

Bathing Beauties

Sun-Kissed

Sunny Side Up

Itsy Bitsy Teenie Weenie Bikini

Hot! Hot! Hot!

Sun Goddess

Toasted Buns

Beached

Swimsuit Model in Training

Bikini Babe

FRIED

Feel the Burn

HOT! HOT! HOT!

OUCH

SIZZLE

Too Hot to Handle

Well-Done

BAKING

sunrise/sunset

Serenity

Breathtaking

Blaze on the Horizon

The Break of Day

A Beautiful Beginning to a Beautiful Day

A Beautiful Ending

A New Day Dawns

---

surfing

Body Surfing

Hangin' On for Dear Life

Hangin' Ten

Getting Wave Reviews

The Blue Crush

What a Rush!

A Wave of Excitement

Working the Waves

Whoa!

TIP
For a playful look, apply the letters in a crooked manner.

TOP TITLES and TIPS TOO!

Surf's Up

Catch a Wave

---

swimming

Dive In

Itsy Bitsy Teenie Weenie Bikini

Bikini Babe

Little Mermaid

Staying Cool in the Pool

SPLASH!

A Splashin' Good Time

Makin' Waves

Man Overboard

Wet 'N' Wild

Off the Deep End

Water, Water Everywhere

Water World

Pool School

Our Little Fish

Just Add Water

Sink or Swim

I Rule the Pool!

TOP TITLES and TIPS TOO!

Don't be Afraid to Get Your Feet Wet

A Real Lifesaver

Staying Afloat

Swim Meet

Water Bug

GET WET

Coolin' Off

Water Whimsy

H2Oh!

Swimsuit Model in Training

---

swing

Just-a-Swinging

Higher! Higher!

Up, Up and Away

Look at Me

A Spring Swing

Swing into Summer

Set Your Sights High

Rock-a-Bye Baby

Swing By Sometimes

Sky High

Getting Into the Swing of Things

Talking

(see also Firsts)

From the Mouths of Babes...

From the Mouths of Babes Comes Truth

Just Say the Word

Blah Blah Blah

A Man of Few Words

Speaker of the House

A Tiny Voice

VOCAL

That's What I Thought You Said

The Most Precious Sound

Kids Say the Darnest Things

Small Talk

Baby Babble

Wit & Wisdom from a 3 year-old

TOP TITLES and TIPS TOO!

Babble On

A Language All His Own

Sweet Talk

Let's Talk

Speaking Sarah-ese

Girl Talk

Toddler Talk

Say It Like It Is

A Word to the Wise

Look Who's Talking

Hearing Voices

You Don't Say?

Talk to Me

Motor Mouth

The Mouth of the South

Gossip, Gossip, Gossip

Let's Talk About It

Say What?

Goo Goo DA DA (substitute your child's first word)

Teacher/Teaching

Teachers Touch Tomorrow

Teaching is a Work of Heart

In Teaching Others, We Teach Ourselves -proverb

Thank You, Ma'am

Teddy Bear

The Bear Necessities

Someone Beary Special

Grin and Bear It

Please Bear With Me

I Love You Beary Much

Bear-y Special

Bear-ly 2 years old

As Cuddly as a Teddy Bear

G-R-O-W-L

GRIZZLY

TIP
When using a single photo on your layout, arch the title above or below for a framing effect.

TOP TITLES and TIPS TOO!

Teddy & Me

I'm Stuffed

Teenager

WHATEVER

Hangin' Out

Rebel Without A Cause

Always My Baby

Boys to Men

Earth to Brandon!

Teen Scene

Just BeTeen Us

When Good Kids Go Teen

Hold Me Close, Let Me Go

A Rose in Bloom

A Work in Progress

TIP
Title a page with a slang word or phrase, often used by your teenager.

TEETH

Tooth or Dare

Sweet Tooth

Toothless in Seattle

Pickin' and Grinnin'

Show Us Those Pearly Whites

Brace Yourself

Ol' Toothless

The Ruthless, The Toothless

The Missing Link

Good, Clean Fun

Spoiled Rotten

Dear Tooth Fairy, (tell the story behind the lost tooth or write a letter to the Tooth Fairy describing the reaction to the visit)

Snaggletooth

Just a Little Bit

TIP

Use a quote from your child. For example, if your child has lost a tooth, use a quote about losing the tooth or something said about the Tooth Fairy.
Example: All I Got Was A Dollar!

TOP TITLES and TIPS TOO!

Dental Health

All the Better to Bite You With!

Telephone

HELLO?

Close Call

RING RING RING

Say What?

Let's Talk About It

Gossip Gossip Gossip

What Did We Do Before Call Waiting?

Tennis

(see also Sports)

Grand Slam Trainee

What's All the Racquet About

Tennis, Anyone?

I "Love" Tennis

Tennis Ace

Serious Tennis

Tennis is My Racquet

Thanksgiving

THANKS

A Time for Thanks

What a Turkey!

THANKFUL

Holidaze

Turkey Time

A Thanksgiving Feast

Blessed Are We

Harvest of Happiness

Stuffed like a Thanksgiving Turkey

STUFFED

Howdy Pilgrim

An Abundance of Blessings

Time

Where Did the Time Go?

The Passage of Time

TOP TITLES and TIPS TOO!

Time Lapse

Time-Out

Wait and See

Well Worth the Wait

The Sands of Time

Take Your Time

How Did It Get So Late, So Early?

Time Flies When You're Having Fun

If We Could Freeze Time...

A Timeless Beauty

Then and Now

Travel Back in Time

Time Heals All Wounds

Perfect Timing

Father Time

Wait a Minute

Ready, Set, Wait

TIP

Put clock hands inside the o's in your title, or use clock hands in place of i's. Also, this could be a good place to do a timeline layout, showing the progression of a subject or event over a period of time.

Once Upon a Time...

Somewhere in Time

Now or Never

Time & Again

One Moment in Time

Now's the Time

A Window of Time

Toilet/Toilet Training

It's My Potty, and I'll Cry If I Want To

To Pee Or Not To Pee

Doody Calls

Ready, Set, Go?

Potty Pooper

A Visit to the Powder Room

I'm Pooped

Tinkle, Tinkle, Little Star

Taking Care of Business

Have a Seat

Who Needs Diapers? Not Me!

Oops

I'm a Big Boy Now

…In Training

A King and His Throne

When Ya' Gotta Go, Ya' Gotta Go

Tongue

Tongue Twister

Hey, Good Lickin'

It Takes a Lickin'

Toys

Toys, Toys Everywhere

You Can Never Have Too Many Toys

Look What I've Got

Just a Few of My Favorite Things

I'm Bored

Tip

Does your child have a special name for his favorite toy? Example: My Choo-Choo. Also, try looking up specific toys such as dolls, blocks or construction.

So Many Toys, So Little Time

These are a Few of My Favorite Things

Mine!

Playtime

Peaceful Play

Power Play

A FUNdamental Toy

The Joy Of Having It All

Born to Play

Eat, Sleep, Play

Tradition

A Time-honored Tradition

Rich in Tradition

Here We Go Again

Memorable Moments

Making Memories

Family Tradition

An Annual Event

Same Time, Same Place, Different Year

Train

I Think I Can, I Think I Can, I Can! (This is cute for a child doing something for the first time, such as learning to walk.)

Choo!Choo!

Chew!Chew!

The Little Engine that Could

Imagination Station

Welcome Aboard

Lil' Depot

All Aboard!

Treehouse

No Boys Allowed

No Girls Allowed

Home Away From Home

Home Sweet Wooden Home

Home Sweet Treehouse

TROUBLE

Caught in the Act

Caught Red-Handed

Here Comes Trouble

Who Me?

Trouble is My Middle Name

The Age of Innocence?

Double Trouble

I've Been Framed!

Wild Child

Partners in Crime

Riot Act

The Truth Will Set You Free

Spoiled Rotten

Busted!

Boy, Are You In Trouble!

Whodunnit

The Scene of the Crime

The Devil Made Me Do It

Oops

Is This Legal?

Hang Your Troubles Out To Dry

I Didn't Do It

The Usual Suspect

Problem Child

I'm a Real Handful

On the Wrong Side of the Law

Troublemaker

ultrasound

(see also baby)

Already Adorable

The Inside Story

My Womb-mate

Here I Am!

Look Out World, Here I Come

---

uncle

Being an Uncle Means…

Monkey's Uncle

My Buddy, My Uncle

It's All Relative

Uncle Unique

My Uncle Rules!

The World's Best Uncle

vacation/traveling

(see also Driving and Airplane)

Road Trip

On the Road Again

PARADISE

Our Paradise

Our Escape

The Great Escape

No Direction in Life

Going the Extra Mile

Are We There Yet?

What a Trip!

Far From Home

Far & Away

The Weary Traveler

Wish You Were Here

TOP TITLES and TIPS TOO!

Island Hopping

Head for the Hills

Travel Companions

How Much Longer?

Family Time

Family Retreat

A Mountain Retreat

Goin' Places

Rest and Relaxation

Miles of Smiles

The Time of Our Lives

World Travelers

TOURISTS

Professional Tourists

Getting There is Half the Fun

Northern Exposure

TIP
Create the appearance of a ransom note using leftover alphabet stickers. Use this on a page about a visit from someone special, saying you're never letting him or her go.

Up North

Southern Charm

Southern Hospitality

Begin Your Journey

Valentine's Day

Happy Love Day

Sweet Somethings

CUPID

Be Mine

Be My Valentine

A Day for Love

Thanks Cupid!

My Favorite Valentine

My Funny Valentine

TIP
Title this page with a phrase from a special Valentine you received. If there is room, include the card on the page.

VOLLEYBALL

(see also Sports)

SPIKE!

Bump, Set, Spike!

ROTATE

Volunteer

A Labor of Love

Changing Lives

Do What You Like, Like What You Do

Making the World a Better Place

Touching Lives

Walk/Walking

(see also Firsts)

First Steps

Look Mom! No Hands!

One Step at a Time

Do the Two Step

Walking on Sunshine

Walking on Cloud Nine

Every Step of the Way

Walk This Way

These Feet Were Made for Walking

A Step in the Right Direction

Get Movin'

There's a Spring in My Step

In Step with Connie

Pitter Patter

Baby in Motion

On the Move

Up and Running

Steppin' Out in Style

Sole Searching

Baby on the Loose!

On the Go

High Steppin'

Get a Move On, Baby

Stepping Out in the World

A Quiet Stroll

Sweetness in Motion

Lil' Rambler

A Walk to Remember

TOP TITLES and TIPS TOO!

Ready, Set, Walk!

Goin' Places

STROLLIN'

Take a Stroll

Step-by-Step

Step by Tiny Step

Going, Going, GONE

Look Out World, Here I Come

Put Your Best Foot Forward

---

war

(see military)

---

watermelon

A Taste of Summer

A Slice of Life

---

wedding/marriage

(see also love)

I Do

Just Married

Happily Ever After

Always and Forever

A Dream Come True

Breathtaking Beauty

A Day to Remember

Our Wedding Day

To Have & To Hold

A Vision in White

Wedded Bliss

Everlasting

The Happy Couple

Together Forever

Just the Beginning

Here Comes the Bride

A Life as One

A Marriage Made in Heaven

Mr. & Mrs.

A Blessed Union

Two Hearts, One Love

The Best Day of My Life

I Wish You Eternity

FOREVER

window

The Window to My Soul

The Window to My World

A Window of Opportunity

Reflections

Window of Time

I Spy

Waiting

Looking Glass

---

women

The Queen

Anything Man Can Do, I Can Do Better

Super Woman

Girls Will Be Girls

Women Will Be Girls

Classic Beauties

---

work

I Owe! I Owe! Off to Work I Go

Waiting for the Weekend

A Labor of Love

Every Mother is a Working Woman

Working Together

Do What You Like, Like What You Do

T.G.I.F.

My Associates, My Friends

Opportunity Knocks

Business as Usual

A Hard Day's Work

It's All in a Day's Work

Another Day, Another Dollar

All Work, No Play

Back to Work

Who's the Boss?

World

What Goes Around, Comes Around

On Top of the World

It's a Small World After All

Joy to the World

Making the World a Better Place

Children Make the World a Magical Place

TOP TITLES and TIPS TOO!

The Eighth Wonder of the World

Like Nothing Else on Earth

The World is My Stage

Heaven on Earth

A World of Personality

Out of this World!

World Leader

Ruling the World!

World's Happiest Couple

World's Best Kid

As the World Turns

---

worm

WIGGLE WIGGLE WIGGLE

The Early Bird Gets the Worm

Squirmy Worm

---

wreck
(see also driving)

Just Call Me Crash

Bumper Cars

Hittin' the Road (& the Mailbox)

Oops

A Nervous Wreck

wrestling

World's Wackiest Friends

Show No Mercy

Take Down

PINNED

Rough and Tumble

Roughhousing

yard

Lawn Ranger

Ready, Set, Mow

Backyard Buddies

Backyard Beauties

Yard Animals

Yard Art(ists)

TOP TITLES and TIPS TOO!

Grasshoppers

Outdoor Fun

Yard Dwellers

Barefoot & Fancy Free

The Great Outdoors

ScrapYard

Yard Work

The Grass Is Always Greener

Wide Open Spaces

Nature Boy

In or Out!

Mowing vs. Growing

The Essence of Summer

The Backyard Boys

Backyard Bonanza

Let's Go Outside

Playin' Hard in the Yard

Yard Sale

Memories for a Quarter

Cherished Memories: 50¢

Trash to Treasure

Bargain Hunters

Bargain Bonanza!

---

yell/yelling

Ahhhhhh!!!

The Call of the Wild

Shout it from the Rooftops

I Scream, You Scream, We All Scream

ZOO

Lions, Tigers, and Bears...Oh, My!

Do the Zoo

Safari, So Good

Our Trip to the Zoo

Feedin' Time at the Zoo

Ever Feel Caged?

What a Zoo

WILDLIFE

TOP TITLES and TIPS TOO!

The Call of the Wild

It's a Jungle Out There

An Elephant Never Forgets (record the memories that you hope to never forget)

Do Not Feed the Animals

Petting Zoo

You're Lion to Me!

Wild Child

Wild Thang

A Wild Day

Strange & Exotic-I'm Strange, the Animals are Exotic

_____

_____

TOP TITLES and TIPS TOO!

ADDITIONAL TITLES

ADDITIONAL TITLES

ADDITIONAL TITLES

TOP TITLES and TIPS TOO!

ADDITIONAL TITLES